The Wolseley Helmet In Pictures From Omdurman To El Alamein

by Stuart Bates
with Peter Suciu

PSB Publishing
Melbourne, Australia
and New York, USA.
www.militarysunhelmets.com

ISBN 978-0-9806567-0-1

Design, layout and editing by Stuart Bates.
Copy by Stuart Bates and Peter Suciu.

Cover design by Nick Jenkin.

Rear cover: Vanity Fair cartoon of Garnet Wolseley, 1874
(Collection of Stuart Bates).

Printed and bound in China

Table of Contents

Foreword

Over the years nothing has identified the colonial soldier more than his sun helmet. This was especially true for the British 'Tommy' of the Victorian era. The sun helmet, variously known as a pith helmet or topi, was not limited to soldiers of the Crown. A number of countries, many of whom were members of the British Commonwealth but also countries with no historical ties or political allegiance to Britain wore sun helmets of one pattern or another.

However, the pattern most widely used in the early to mid-20th century was undeniably of British influence, and whether he had a hand in its design or not, has since been inextricably identified with Field Marshal Wolseley whose name was officially attached to it in the 1900 *Dress Regulations,* for the West African Regiment and the Chinese Regiment only, and extended to all regiments/corps abroad in the 1904 *Dress Regulations*.

This pattern is a logical design evolution of the white Foreign Service helmet which identified the British soldier on campaign and which has been immortalized in films such as *Zulu*. The Wolseley continues to be worn today by the Royal Marines as well as by a number of regiments throughout the world.

The authors, who previously co-authored *Military Sun Helmets of the World*, have brought together a remarkable sampling of "Wolseleys" from around the world. Working primarily from their own comprehensive collections they have located additional rare examples for inclusion as well as contemporary photographs of the helmet in wear. Combined, this photographic study offers the collector the first reference dedicated to this unique item of headdress.

Clive M. Law
October, 2009

Acknowledgements

The authors would like to express their thanks to the following for their assistance in the preparation of this book: Michael Barthorp, Pedro Soares Branco, David Ford, Dave Gerardi, James Howell, Ron Kidd, Jim MacDonald, Peter Payne, David Read, Peter Verstraeten-Vlerick.

Photos of the Gloucestershire Regiment courtesy of the Soldiers of Gloucestershire Museum.

Punch cartoon reproduced with the permission of Punch Ltd., www.punch.co.uk

Vanity Fair cartoon an original lithograph from the collection of Stuart Bates.

A great debt is owed to Jon Mills, a published author of British military uniforms and insignia, and editor of the *Formation Sign* magazine of the Military Heraldry Society. Jon contributed much invaluable information and many period photos in addition to the photo of his Duke of Wellington's Regiment Wolseley helmet.

To Gordon Byrne, Jon Mills and David Wanless go thanks for their invaluable insights and assistance, as well as their proof reading of this book.

Keith Matthews, Curator of Military History, York Museums Trust (York Castle Museum), contributed his expertise and many photos of the experimental Wolseley helmets featured in this book.

Thanks to Ron Kidd, Col. Dudley Wall, Col. Will Endley and Andrew Dinnes for their invaluable contributions to the South African chapter.

Clive M. Law, who wrote the foreword, is a well-known Canadian militaria author and publisher of books on the Canadian military experience as seen through its material culture. In his spare time he collects Canadian military headdress. Clive also contributed the photos of Canadian helmets and period photos in addition to providing invaluable information on the Canadian adoption of the Wolseley.

A special thanks to my friend and professional photographer, Nick Jenkin, who photographed most of the helmets for this book and for his skill and patience in editing every photo used. Nick was also responsible for the cover design.

Stuart Bates
October, 2009

Introduction

The Story of the Sun Helmet Continues

The subject of sun helmets, also commonly known as pith helmets, is one that has not been covered in much detail. Despite the fact that these helmets were used throughout the world by most of the major powers of Europe, South America and even by the United States for more than 100 years this form of military headgear is often overlooked. Sun helmets fall neither into the category of true combat helmets or dress headgear - yet this unique form of cover has been used at times in both a combat and ceremonial role.

This book is meant not to serve as a follow-up to *Military Sun Helmets of the World*, but rather as a supplement and companion. Instead of covering the topic in broad strokes and touching upon key elements from around the world, Stuart Bates and I have opted to focus on just one particular pattern of helmets. This is the British Wolseley helmet, which was introduced when the Empire was essentially at its zenith, but at a point where military planners should have clearly seen that one age was ending and another was beginning.

Thus while the Wolseley has a moniker that evokes an eminent Victorian general, it is in fact a helmet more accurately associated with the First and Second World Wars. Instead of being the helmet of empire builders, the Wolseley pattern helmet was worn by the guardians of the Empire. Thus with respect to author Byron Farwell, this was not the helmet of Mr. Kipling's army but essentially Mr. Churchill's armies.

From the Battle of Omdurman to the Gallipoli campaign, to the Battle of El Alamein the Wolseley was there. It may not have been the dominant form of headgear in any of these battles, but it was there. From the Boer War to the Palestine Front in 1917 and even to the final campaign under the shadow of the Sphinx in 1942 the Wolseley pattern sun helmet had its place.

The helmet pattern was popular, and widely copied, used by friend and foe alike. Yet it is a helmet that few have written about, and one that is often misrepresented by collectors and dealers. Even today the helmet remains in limited use, by bandsmen and some territorial police forces. More importantly as a piece of history, this helmet pattern serves as a reminder of "the fight for England's glory." Collectors, such as Stuart and I, have a special appreciation for this helmet, and thus our desire to tell its story. And like the Soldiers of the Queen, we're not letting it fade away or gradually die.

This book is by no means meant to be the definitive work on the subject, and the authors sincerely trust that much additional information will come to light through its publication.

Peter Suciu
October, 2009

Chapter 1
The Wolseley Helmet

PUNCH'S FANCY PORTRAITS.—No. 96.

SIR GARNET WOLSELEY.

Short Service and Quick Returns.

Field Marshal Garnet Joseph Wolseley, 1st Viscount Wolseley KP GCB OM GCMG VD PC, to give him his full title, was considered by many to be the greatest General of the late Victorian period. Indeed, the phrase "everything's all Sir Garnet", meaning "all is in order" was coined because of his reputation for efficiency.

Born in 1833, Wolseley served in Burma, the Crimean War, the Indian Mutiny, China, Canada, the Zulu War, the Sudan and in West Africa where his brilliantly conducted Ashanti Campaign in 1873-74 was considered a model of efficiency, as was his Red River Campaign in Canada of 1870.

Wolseley was known for selecting the ablest and best soldiers of his day, the so-called "Wolseley Ring", and was a keen advocate of the short service regime which required men to serve for 12 years, divided into active and reserve service, rather than for "life". This brought him into conflict with the "traditionalists" headed by the Duke of Cambridge, then Commander-in-Chief of the British Army. Wolseley also came into conflict with the "Indian" faction headed by Field Marshal Sir Frederick Roberts and it has been said that he had a "jealousy of all Indian officers." [1]

Sir Garnet Wolseley was a stickler for preparation and intelligence-gathering before embarking on his campaigns. He often sent officers to the area of proposed conflict well in advance of a campaign's beginning and in the Red River Campaign even supervised the details of the loading of individual boats. He did, however, give great latitude to his staff in the area of logistics, but was ruthless when they failed in their duties.

Origins of the Wolseley Helmet

The origins of the Wolseley helmet are shrouded in mystery although it appears, on the photographic record, first in the 1896-98 campaign in the Sudan. Lord Kitchener, who was greatly troubled by the glare of the desert sun such that his eyesight became permanently impaired, readily adopted the helmet and it was soon taken up by General and Staff officers. However, its use by Field Officers in the Boer War, 1899-1902, was somewhat curtailed by the accuracy of the Boers' marksmanship.

It was variously known as the "Kitchener" or "Egyptian" pattern and was only first officially referred to as the Wolseley in the *Dress Regulations for the Army 1900* but was mandated for the West African and Chinese Regiments, and only in khaki. [2]

As late as 1925, according to Regimental Standing Orders, the 8th King George V's Own Light Cavalry were to wear plain "Kitchener" helmets. [3] *Also of interest is that the 1904 Dress Regulations refer to it as the "Egyptian" pattern as well as the "Wolseley."*

How the helmet acquired the name of Wolseley can only be a matter of conjecture. However it must be remembered that Sir Garnet Wolseley was at this time Commander-in-Chief of the Army and took an active interest in such matters.

A Colonial pattern helmet illustrating the steep front peak and rear brim and the lack of sun protection on the temples.

Colonial Pattern Helmet

The Colonial pattern helmet, which held sway until the first decade of the 20th century, was long criticised for the lack of sun protection to the temples and the difficulties imposed by the steep front and rear peaks on firing a rifle in the prone position or laying a cannon. Indeed the 1900 Dress Regulations on page 74 states:

> **Officers should be careful that their Tradesmen do not supply them with "smart" looking helmets instead of those capable of affording protection from the sun. In fitting themselves with helmets, they should take care that the back part comes well down so as to shield the back of the neck, and that the temples are well covered. The sealed pattern should be strictly adhered to.**

A *Vanity Fair* magazine caricature of Wolseley which appeared in 1874 (Collection of Stuart Bates).

This *Vanity Fair* caricature of Wolseley, published in 1874, further muddies the waters as it shows a helmet with considerable flare to the front peak and side brims. Far more than the patterns of helmets that were in widespread use for the British Army overseas of the time.

This could be attributed to artistic licence but could indicate that officers, especially General officers, may have been instrumental in affecting the design of headgear and other elements of uniform and equipment that would enhance the efficiency of the British soldier. This would not be unexpected of Wolseley who was known for his predilection for thorough planning and supply.

Experimental Helmets Prior to the Wolseley

Experimental helmets, to replace the Colonial pattern Foreign Service Helmet, were being trialled by the British Army from, at least, the late 1880s. A photograph of the 1st Battalion, Northamptonshire Regiment taken in 1892 shows them wearing an experimental white helmet which had flared front, side and rear peaks. However, this helmet was not taken into service. [4]

This enlargement from the Northamptonshire photo clearly shows the style changes from the Colonial pattern.

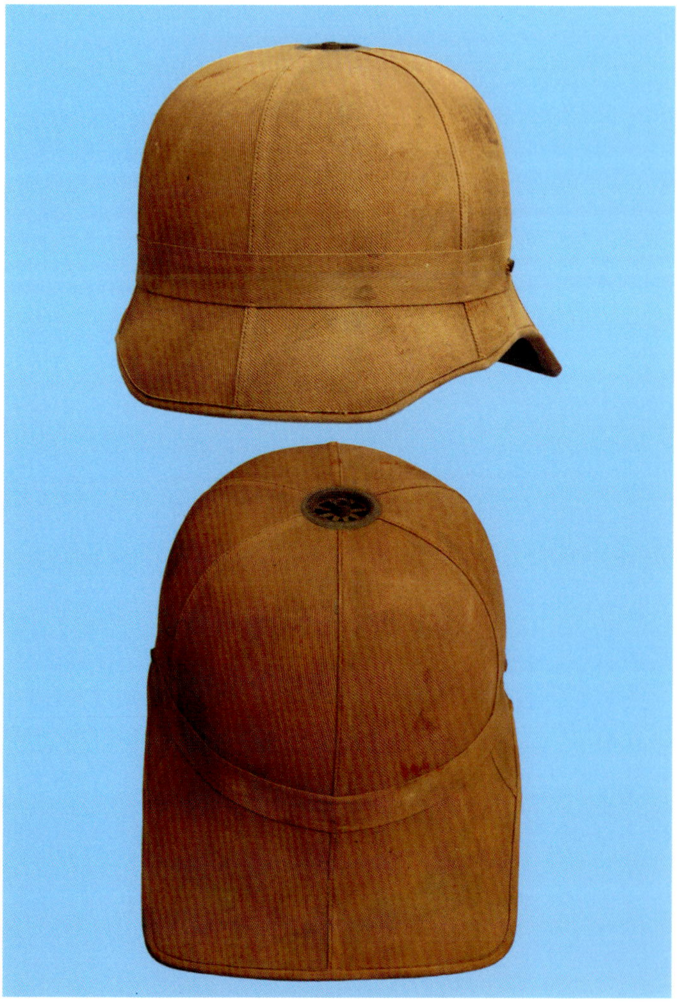

An extremely rare rank and file experimental helmet dated 1896 made by Hawkes & Co. This helmet was not taken into service and only two survivors are known to exist. This example was found in a garage in the village of Banwell, Somerset, U.K.

The 1st Battalion of the Northamptonshire Regiment photographed in 1892 on manoeuvres. They are wearing an experimental white helmet introduced in the late 1880s (Courtesy of Michael Barthorp).

A side view of the 1896 experimental helmet showing the distinctive German influence. The reason for the rippling side brim remains unknown and gives no more protection from the sun than the Colonial pattern helmet.

The interior view of the 1896 experimental helmet showing the Hawkes & Co. maker's ink stamp.

A top view of the 1896 experimental helmet. Note the removal of the ventilator cap and side rosettes prior to de-commissioning.

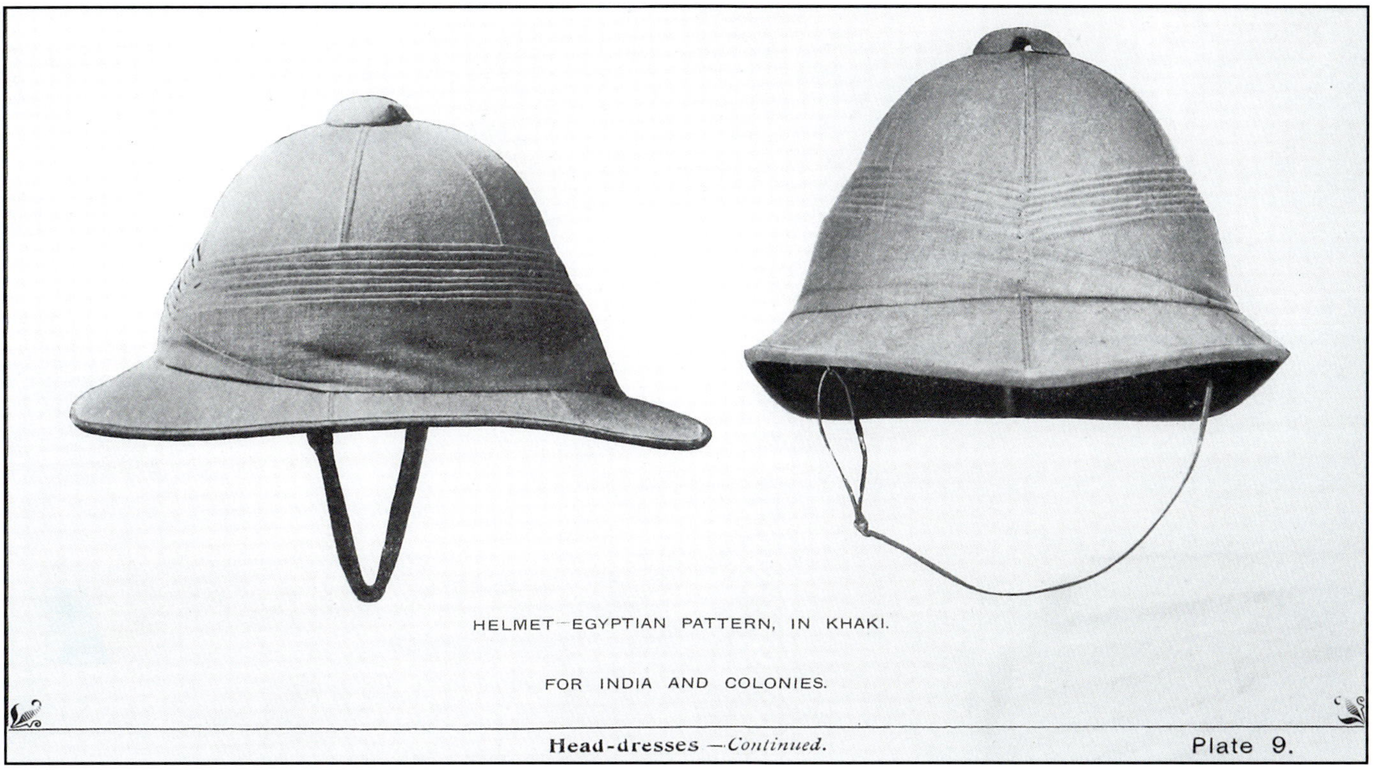

The Wolseley helmet as pictured in the 1904 Dress Regulations for Officers of the Army (Collection of Stuart Bates).

At least one other pattern, described on previous pages, was considered and the two surviving helmets of this pattern indicate that it wasn't just a simple transition from Colonial to Wolseley pattern.

Specification

The Wolseley helmet became a "sealed pattern" in September, 1899. The sealed pattern for any article was the model which all manufacturers were required to duplicate in their manufacturing process, however, differences appeared over time e.g. rounded or pointed front peaks, taller crowns and curled rear brim.

The 1900 Dress Regulations defines the Wolseley helmet, for officers, in paragraph 773 as -

773. Helmet -- "Wolseley" pattern, cork covered with khaki, made with six seams, bound buff leather, projecting peak all round, 3 inches wide in front, 4 inches at back, and 2 inches at the sides, ventilated at top with zinc-covered button, side hooks with leather chin strap.

The helmet was covered in khaki drill cotton and usually lined with green cotton and was mandated for the West African and Chinese Regiments only. Other Ranks' helmets were bound with khaki drill or webbing tape as opposed to the buff leather specified for officers.

It was almost always fitted with a puggaree, a cloth wrapping, normally cotton, around the dome and was up to 24ft (7.4m) long. [5] It had a variable number of pleats; from as few as three to as many as twelve, including piping.

The puggaree was usually flipped at the front and rear, however several regiments had different arrangements with three or even four points at which the cloth was flipped. For example, the Suffolks had a three flipped puggaree - one on either side and one at the front. [6] The Cameronians (Scottish Rifles) had the puggaree flipped at four points - the front, rear and both sides. [7]

Its original purpose was to keep the wearer's head cool and to provide protection from a sword cut, but how effective it was in these capacities is open to debate.

A side view of the Wolseley helmet.

A rear view of the Wolseley helmet.

The Wolseley helmet began unofficially replacing the Colonial Helmet in 1901 and was in general use at the start of World War I, seeing service in the Gallipoli, Middle East and African campaigns. As most of the helmets produced for these campaigns were khaki, a white cover was never considered. [8]

A front view of the Wolseley helmet.

According to Pattern Books of the Royal Army Clothing Factory, Pimlico, a "Standard" i.e. "sealed" pattern was deposited for a white drill Wolseley on 15th December 1903, followed two weeks later by a khaki cover. Another entry in the Pattern Books states, on 23rd March 1904, a khaki helmet should be universally adopted for all dress abroad but "Owing to the large number of reserves of the white helmet... no new pattern could come into use for about four years." This indicates an astonishing number of white helmets produced in the short space of three years, unless stores of the white Colonial pattern are included.

The 1904 Dress Regulations define the Wolseley as

706. Wolseley pattern, cork covered with khaki drill, made with six seams, bound buff leather, projecting peak all round, 3 inches in front, 4 inches at back, and 2 inches at the sides, ventilated at top with zinc button covered with khaki drill, side hooks. At top of helmet a collet riveted on to a collar 3/8 inch wide to receive button, brown leather chin strap, 3/8 inch wide. Plumes, spikes, chin-chains, etc., will be worn on ceremonial occasions when not on duty with the troops.

Additionally these Dress Regulations stipulate that it was for service at all stations abroad, another case of the official Dress Regulations catching up with reality. [9] The 1911 Dress Regulations has the helmets in white or khaki drill, but the khaki helmet with a white cover and white puggaree may be substituted for the white helmet. [10]

As with the Colonial Helmet, the Wolseley was typically worn without spike, plates or other accoutrements unless on full dress occasions and then on the white helmet only. Even as late as the 1934 Dress Regulations this restriction was still in force but regimental patches (flashes) were allowed to be worn on the khaki version, as well as plumes, hackles and regimental badges for selected regiments.

A top view of the Wolseley helmet.

The Wolseley was also sometimes fitted with a neck curtain, as was its predecessor, but this item was discontinued in 1921. The cleverer soldiers often purchased an extra chinstrap - the one to be worn over the brim and the other under the chin - to save constant alteration of the length of the chinstrap depending on how it was required to be worn.

Materials and Construction

The helmet was originally specified as being of cork covered with drill cotton, but wartime exigencies forced manufacturers to look for alternative materials.

Cork is primarily sourced from the **cork oak** (Quercus suber) which requires plenty of sun, low rainfall and high

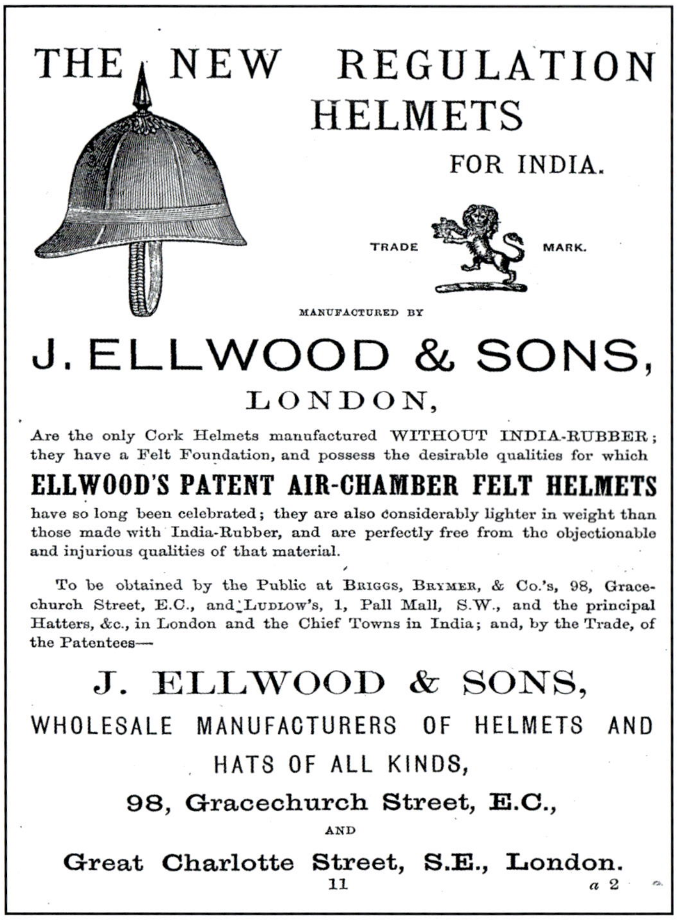

An advert from the 1877 India List for a cork and felt helmet (Courtesy www.youroldbooksandmaps.co.uk).

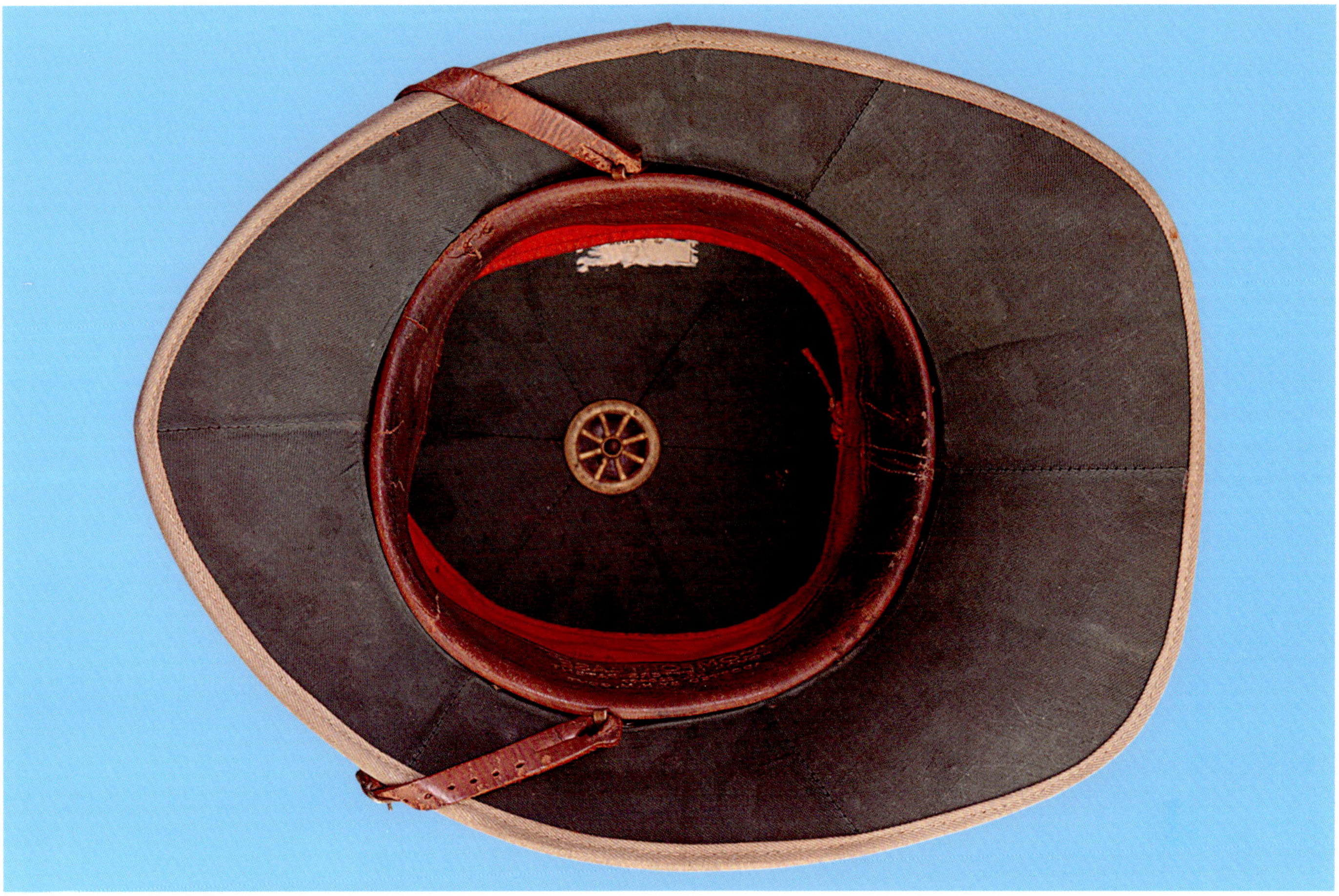

The interior of a cork Wolseley showing the green cotton lining most common in these helmets.

The interior of a straw Wolseley also showing the green cotton lining in these helmets. Note the four tabs on the ventilation cap which are bent over to secure that cap. The straw construction would not support the normal screw in ventilator cap and collet.

The interior of a felt Wolseley showing the green felt lining in these helmets. Aluminium or tin foil was used at times as a heat shield to the crown interior but its effectiveness is debatable.

humidity and such conditions are readily found along the coast of the Mediterranean Sea.

Cork has a unique set of properties. It is lightweight yet strong, rot resistant, fire resistant, termite resistant, is soft and buoyant and impermeable to gas and liquid.

It contains a natural waxy substance called **suberin** which makes cork impermeable to liquids and therefore an ideal material for a tropical helmet.[11]

Officers' cork helmets were of three-ply construction i.e. two thin sheets of cork with a cloth material glued between. It is probable that the Other Ranks' were of a cheaper construction with only a single layer of cork and material.

During the First World War, because of the cost and difficulty of obtaining cork, straw was used as a substitute material. Helmets made from this material were quite strong and two are known to exist today and are part of the collection of one of the authors.

A third material used was felt, which had long been used in hat and, therefore, helmet making but was replaced by cork as the preferred material by the British Army in the late 19th century. The 1877 advert shown previously is interesting in that it describes a helmet manufactured from both cork and felt.

Felt Wolseleys appear to be mainly of the Second World War period and, once again, probably because of the difficulty and cost of obtaining supplies of cork.

Helmets made of pith were used in India at least as early as the middle of the 19th century and the Cawnpore Tent Club hat, in particular, became very popular with officers after the Prince of Wales' visit in 1875-76. Pith helmets were used in conjunction with Wolseleys until Army Council Instruction 284 of July 1938 replaced the

The ventilator cap which screwed into the collet at the top of the crown. These caps had three vents.

The eight spoke cartwheel design collet for ventilation through the top of the helmet. Collets with four spokes were used but proved to be a little fragile.

Wolseley and Cawnpore helmets by the Khaki Solar Pith Hat. Wolseleys and Cawnpores already in possession were allowed to be worn until December 31, 1938.[12]

However, the Wolseley continued to be the regulation helmet for stations other than India.

Ventilation

Ventilation was provided by two systems. The first was through the ventilator cap to the top of the helmet. A collet was fixed to the inside top of the crown to allow airflow out of the helmet top. Into this collet was screwed a zinc button usually covered with khaki drill. The button had three vent holes to allow the air to escape. The Worcestershire Regiment differed from all others by having a green painted cap, although this created

The corrugated buckram separating the headband from the shell.

problems when exposed to the sun's heat. When the white helmet was worn, for ceremonial occasions, the spike with base or cup and ball with base was screwed into the collet in place of the button ventilator.

The straw and felt examples were not strong enough to take the metal collet and a cap with four metal tabs was used where the tabs were inserted into the hole at the top

The eight cork spacers between the headband and the helmet shell are clearly shown here.

An interior shot which shows the metal strips separating the headband from the shell.

The leather strips are sewn onto or riveted to the headband and fitted over the metal split pin heads which were passed through the lugs fixed to the helmet shell. This was Vero's Detachable & Self Conforming Headband patented in 1925.

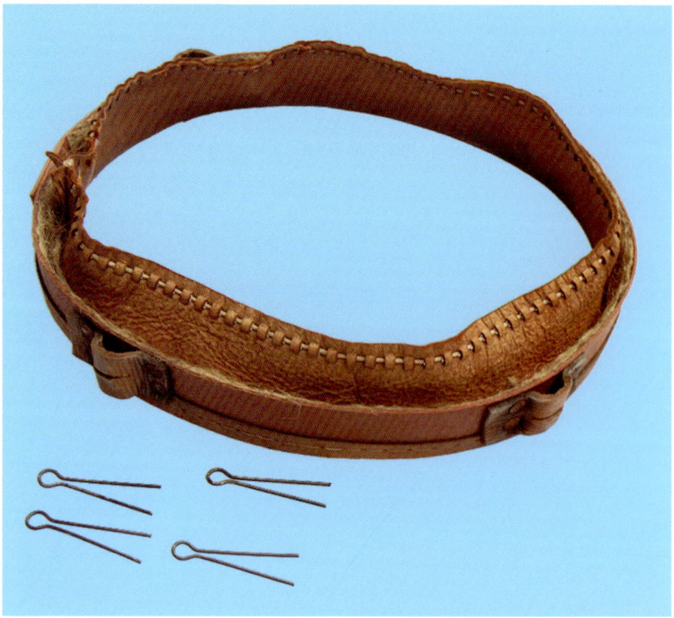

A Vero's Detachable Headband showing the four split pins and the four leather strips used to secure it to the helmet.

of the crown and bent over to secure the button. See the straw and felt examples on previous pages.

The second system of ventilation was to have the leather headband separated from the helmet shell thereby allowing air to flow in between those two components and around the wearer's head.

At least five methods were used to achieve this with the first being the placing of eight cork spacers, more or less, evenly around the headband/shell.

The second was the use of corrugated buckram, or similar material, between the headband and shell. Buckram is a stiff cloth made of cotton. It is impregnated with a starch, which allows it to be softened in water, formed into the required shape and left to dry.

The third method was the fixing of metal strips to the shell to separate it from the headband where the ends were stapled or riveted to the outside of the headband, or attached to a metal band which was inserted into the headband on the helmet shell side. This was patented (number 103425) by Hawkes & Co. and William Charles Bensley, Works Manager, both of 1 Savile Row, London in 1917.

This patent also specified an adjustable leather lining of six leaves which fitted the wearer's head via a drawstring, but this seems to have been used only in steel helmets which are illustrated in the patent application.

The fourth method was to fix metal lugs at four positions around the shell base at 1, 5, 7 and 11 o'clock. Into these lugs were inserted cotter or split pins over which leather strips, sewn or riveted onto the leather headband, would be fitted. This was Vero's Detachable & Self Conforming Headband, Royal Letters Patent No. 228467, of 1925.

An earlier patent (number 207475) was granted to Charles Owen & Co. in 1923. The method used seems to be a series of eyelets around the bottom of the crown and a corresponding series of eyelets in the headband itself. A cord is then threaded through these holes creating not only a space between the shell and the headband but allowing the headband to be fitted to the wearer's head by adjustment of the length of that cord through its ends at the rear of the helmet. That is, a drawstring which pulls the headband clear of the shell and allows for different head sizes.

An example of the Charles Owen & Co. system of separating the helmet shell from the headband.

An unusual drop foil lining showing only two eyelets to provide ventilation between the lining and the helmet crown (Courtesy of York Museums Trust /York Castle Museum).

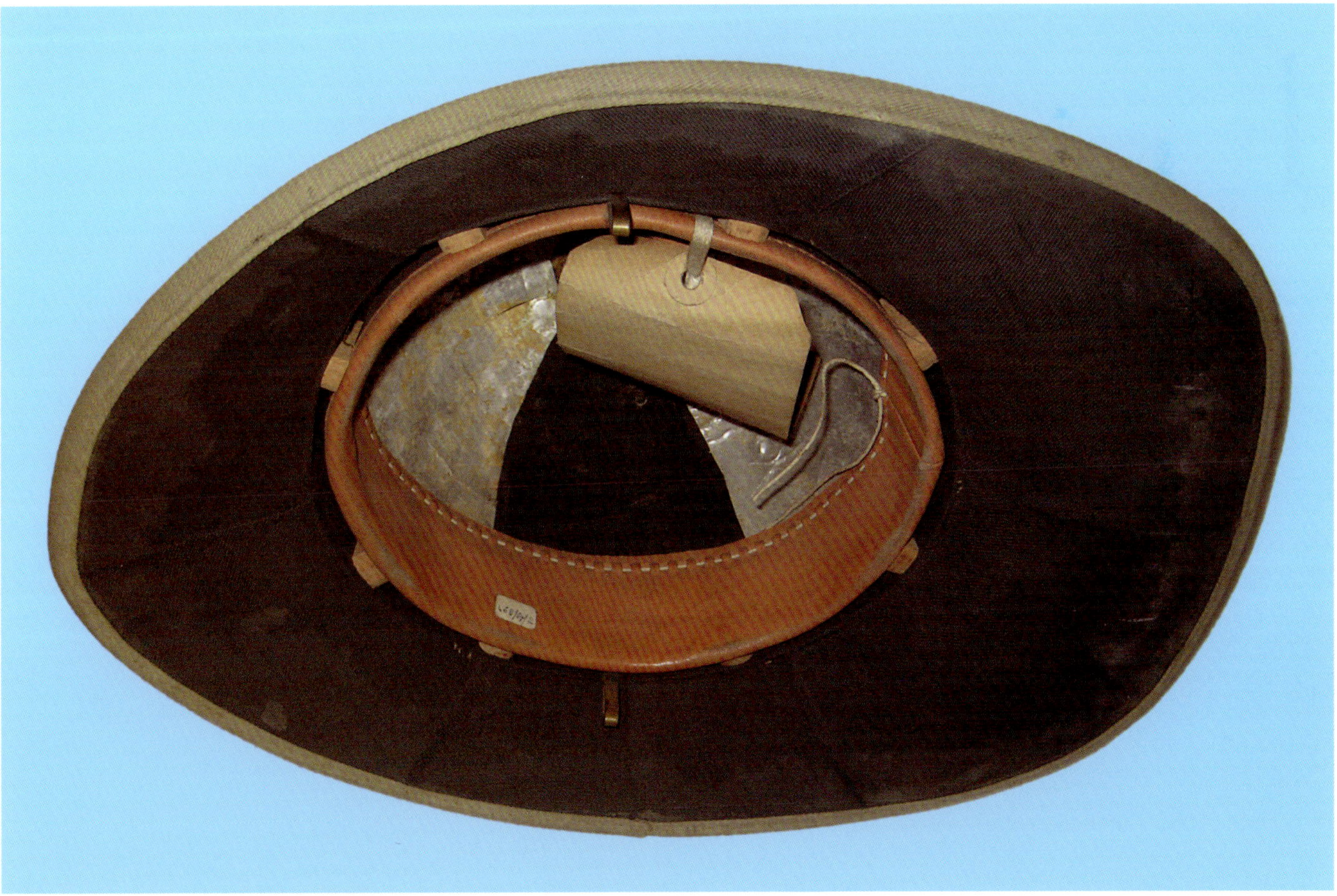

An example of a lining using four metal sheets, with fortunately for the purposes of illustration, one sheet missing. These sheets are not glued to the crown nor are they attached to each other (Courtesy of York Museums Trust /York Castle Museum).

Interior Cooling

Guy Pascoe Crowden took out a patent (number 397985) in 1933 for the application of thin metal foil, usually aluminium or tin, or metal sheets to the interior of the helmet's crown. It is not known how effective this "innovation" was, but a 10-15° Fahrenheit reduction in interior heat was claimed in the patent application.

This aluminium foil lining came in two forms. The first was a single layer glued to the crown shell. This lining was either applied as foil only or had a paper backing. The patent specified that the foil lining could extend to the projecting brim but no examples of this are known to exist.

The second form was called a "dropped lining" which was of a "sandwich" construction with two layers of foil with a stiffening layer of fabric or paper between them. This "sandwich" was "free-floating" and was arranged to allow an air space between the crown of the helmet and the lining and between the lining and the wearer's head. It had a four of eyelets to allow airflow to the top ventilator cap which would otherwise have been completely covered.

These linings were used in conjunction with each other or separately.

This drop lining has four eyelets positioned underneath the top ventilator cap to allow air flow out of the crown of the helmet.

The Royal Army Ordnance Corps Gazette of April 1937 says -

HELMETS (khaki drill)

> **Successful trials have been made of helmets lined with bright aluminium foil to reflect the sun's rays, and further trials will be undertaken shortly of helmets similiarly lined, fitted with detachable head bands, and with a khaki band instead of a pagri (the latter may be superfluous if the foil lining is effective as it promises to be.** [13]

The patent also specified that metal sheets could be substituted for the metal foil attached to the crown. Four sheets of thin metal leaves of a pyrmidal shape are "held in place by their close fitting behind the headband and under the top vent collet, no adhesive is used and the segments are not fixed to each other", says Keith Matthews of York Museums Trust. The photograph on the previous page clearly shows this arrangement.

The drop lining was officially adopted in May 1941, although it is interesting to note that a Wolseley in the York Castle Museum has both foil linings and has a paper label attached which reads "Received P.R. [Pattern Room] 7-7-36..."

HELMETS, UNIVERSAL, KHAKI

> **1. Future supplies of the above-mentioned "Bodies" will be to a changed pattern. It differs from previous pattern in that it has a double lining of aluminium foil...** [14]

It was short-lived because in August 1942 it was dispensed with and "a fixed inner aluminium plain lining" replaced it.

HELMETS, UNIVERSAL, KHAKI

> **The standard pattern of the above-mentioned "Bodies" (B4689, B4699) has been modified to guide future manufacture, in that the aluminium foil drop lining has been dispensed with.**
>
> **Future supplies will only be provided with the fixed inner aluminium plain lining.** [15]

Regimental/Corps Identification

It was commonplace for Regiments and corps to have identifying elements to their helmets. These included flashes affixed to the left side, right side, or both sides of the helmet, as well as hackles of horse/goat's hair or feathers and coloured piping to the pleats of the puggaree. It was not uncommon for officers to wear a flash on both sides while the men only on one side. In some regiments the officers wore only one flash and the men two.

Flashes varied enormously in dimensions and even

The familiar flash of the Royal Artillery.

in design from battalion to battalion of a particular regiment. A British Army regiment of the late Victorian and early Edwardian period typically consisted of two regular battalions, a third and possibly a fourth Militia battalion and a varying number of Volunteer battalions, but this arrangement varied greatly in practice.

This is the third pattern of the flash used by the 7th Armoured Division during their time in North West Europe in WWII. This division was known by the appellation "the Desert Rats" and the animal depicted is the Jerboa or the desert rat.

Piping or a coloured pleat to the folds of a puggaree was another method of distinguishing regiments or corps. For example the Royal Corps of Signals experimented with various flashes and piping to their puggarees. The last used being the corps colours of light blue/dark blue/green at the top of the puggaree. This piping replaced the earlier flash by a directive of the Corps Committee on the 28th May 1937.[16]

This helmet, to the Middlesex Regiment, shows the yellow piping to the top pleat of the puggaree but also the regimental badge on a backing of the regimental colours.

Another distinction used by some regiments was the hackle which was made from cut feathers or horse/goat's hair in the colour of the regiment. For example, the 8th Hussars wore a white over red hackle and the Grenadier Guards regiment a white hackle and for the Coldstream Guards a red hackle.

The white over red horsehair hackle of the 8th Hussars.

Badges were also worn as an identifier of the unit or corps. Badges were worn on the side of the helmet, the front and in the case of the Gloucestershire Regiment on the back of the helmet.

Badges were not allowed to perforate the helmet shell according to the various Dress Regulations, but this rule was honoured as much in the breach as not. The "puggaree badge" had a shaft which slid between the puggaree and the shell but many examples of helmets with badges that perforate the shell are found. Soldiers on overseas duty exercised considerable licence over such matters, even using collar badges on the puggaree.

An example of a slider puggaree badge showing the blade, or shaft which slides between the helmet shell and the puggaree as shown on the next page.

An example of a slider badge fitted to a Wolseley to the Royal Engineers c1937.

Rifle regiments usually had a black leather chinstrap rather than the brown leather for other units. This was in addition to any other distinction.

Full Dress as specified in the Dress Regulations

The white version of the helmet, or the khaki version with white cover and puggaree, was worn on Full Dress occasions such as State Ceremonies, Royal escorts, Guards of Honour, Church parades etc.

The helmet was worn with a spike for infantry, cavalry Royal Engineers and the Army Ordnance Corps, and a ball in a leaf cup ornament to the top for Artillery and other corps. A gilt or gilding metal chinchain replaced the leather chinstrap. For Rifle regiments these items were of blackened bronze. The chinchains, when not worn under the chin, were looped up to a high-hook which was either attached to the top rear of the helmet crown or attached to the spike base.

Plumes were worn by General and Staff officers including Military Secretaries and Aides-de-Camp. These were made of swan feathers of red under white except for Military Secretaries and Aides-de-Camp who wore red over white. Royal Engineer officers and Departmental officers who wore cocked hats wore plumes in the colour prescribed for their respective services.

A full dress Wolseley to the Middlesex Regiment showing the gilt spike and chinchain. This example also has a slider badge on a regimental coloured backing and yellow piping to the top of the puggaree.

A white over red swan feather plume, which being 6 inches in height indicates that it is for officers under the rank of colonel.

The height of plumes varied as follows: for general officers 10 inches; colonels 8 inches and officers under the rank of colonel 6 inches.

A red over white swan feather plume which was worn by Military Secretaries and Aides-de-Camp.

White puggarees were worn with the white helmet or khaki helmet with white cover. The exceptions being a red puggaree for the Duke of Cornwall's Light Infantry, a red and white puggaree for the Northumberland Fusiliers and a buff puggaree for the East Kent Regiment.

This double storage/transit tin accommodates two Wolseley helmets.

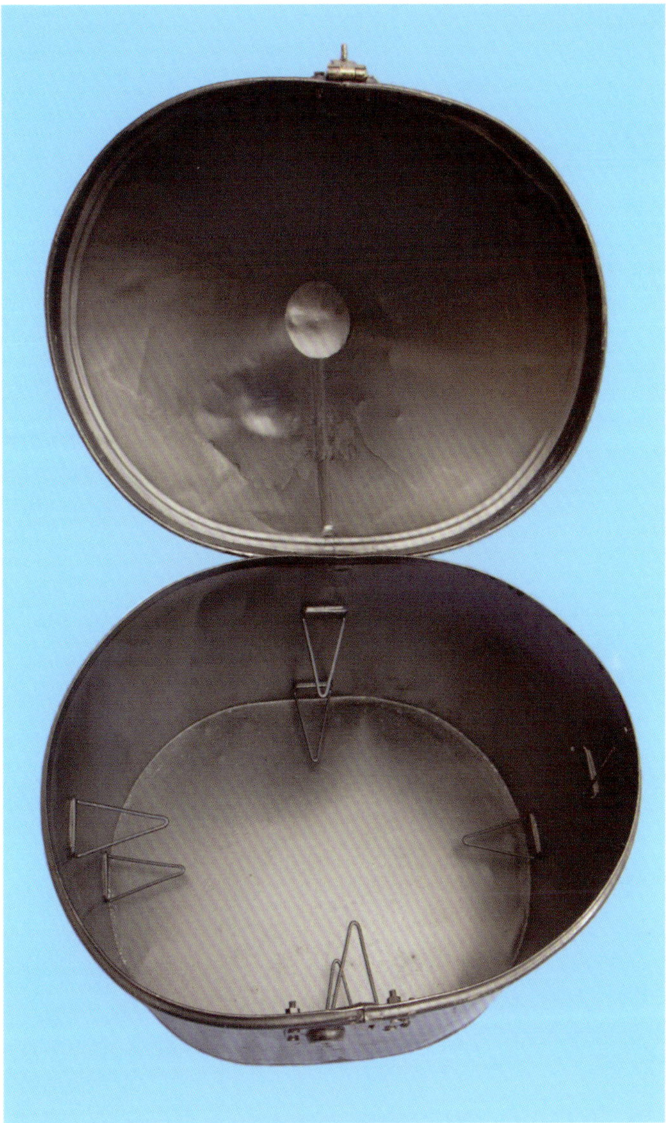

This interior shot of a double tin clearly shows one method of securing the two helmets whilst in transit.

An example of the maker's brass label to a storage/transit tin. This one is to Hawkes & Co., one of the most famous military uniform & accoutrement manufacturers.

A brass plaque to W.E. Huddleston of the Army Medical Staff, renamed as the Royal Army Medical Corps in 1898.

Helmet Tins and Covers

Officers purchased their own helmets and a storage/transit tin often accompanied that purchase. The tin was of a japanned metal construction and versions were made to accommodate a single helmet or two helmets (presumably white and khaki).

Japanning was a process of applying a heavy black lacquer in layers to the metal. Each layer was either allowed to dry naturally or had heat applied. After the last layer the tin was heat dried and polished to give a smooth glossy finish. The lacquer also came in reds, greens and blues, although a dappled red and black finish is the most commonly encountered.

Tins often carried the maker's plaque as shown on the previous page, some also had the name and regiment or corps of the owner - either as a brass plaque or stencilled onto the tin.

The men were issued with cotton covers or bags, fitted with drawstrings, into which the helmet was placed. Very few of these survive and it is quite likely that they were soon discarded by the soldiery.

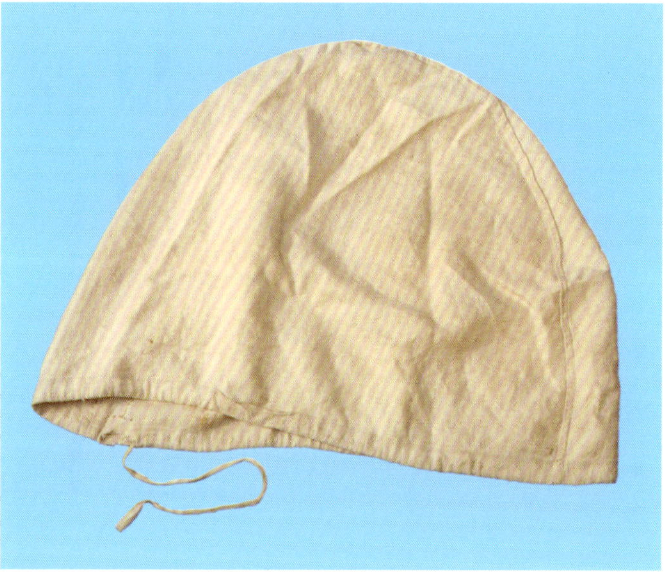

A rare example of a cotton bag issued to Other Ranks to protect their Wolseley helmets when not in use.

Private Purchase and Government Issue

Best quality Foreign Service Hemets purchased by the elite of the officer class were of far superior quality and finish when compared with the Government issue to the other ranks (often known as enlisted men in other countries). Private purchase helmets are usually fitted with a red silk sweatband, attached to a fine leather headband, and less commonly found with cotton mesh sweatbands.

The covering is generally of a fine cotton drill, with a multi-pleat puggaree which is of regimental pattern, and also commonly adorned with the regimental colour flash and/or badge as described earlier.

Premium quality covering may be found by way of "Doeskin" (see Aide-De-Camp helmet in the next chapter), otherwise known as Melton Cloth, a tightly woven woollen cloth, which is heavily milled, and has a nap which is raised to form a short, dense, non-lustrous pile. Melton cloth originated in Melton Mowbray, Leicestershire.

It was also true that there was a good trade in second-hand helmets for those of the officer class who were not financially equipped to buy a new best quality helmet, some resorting to the purchase of the adequate, but lesser quality Government Stores helmet.

Helmets issued to other ranks were manufactured under contract by a number of private companies supplying the Royal Government Clothing Department, Pimlico, and then despatched to the relevant Army Ordnance Clothing depôt for each regiment. [17]

Particular details such as the style of puggaree, colour flash and badge were then addressed at a regimental level.

Where Used and Take-up

The Wolseley, or the Universal Foreign Service Helmet as it was officially known, was worn at all stations abroad and these included: India, Africa, Singapore, the Straits Settlements, Hong Kong, the Sudan, in fact any hot-weather station in which British troops served. It was also used by empire countries such as Australia, Canada, South Africa, New Zealand etc.

The take up of Wolseleys by the British Army was an extended process as the authorities always had a watchful eye on costs. To this end existing stocks of superseded helmets would be issued before the replacement pattern. As Jon Mills says in *From Scarlet To Khaki* -

> **Whilst uniforms were authorised from a certain date, they may not have been immediately adopted. The War Office issued constant reminders not to waste public money, ordering units to wear out old uniforms before taking new items into use. [18]**

It is interesting that the Navy & Army Catalogue of 1907 does not list the Wolseley at all, whilst it does show various pith helmets including the Shikari and the

Navy & Army Catalogue of 1907 (Collection of Stuart Bates).

Cawnpore Tent Club the latter having been used at least as far back as the Prince of Wales' visit to India in 1875.

This would indicate that the Wolseley was not in general use even seven years after its presence was first officially recognised, and three years after it was mandated for all stations abroad - for officers only however. Membership of the Navy & Army Co-operative was restricted to officers and non-commissioned officers, their families and friends at this time.

Lifespan

The Wolseley helmet's life extends from the Sudan Campaign of 1896-98 through to the present day, but 1941 saw the beginning of the end and the authors have never seen a khaki Wolseley dated after 1942.

In 1941 the lovely puggarees of earlier times were officially replaced by a "false" pagri which had a mere three pleats and "Pagris, Khaki" were declared obsolescent. [19]

Signallers of the 2nd Battalion Gloucestershire Regiment in Mesopotamia 1916-1918 (Courtesy Soldiers of Gloucestershire Museum).

In 1942 even this was replaced by a single plain narrow band and the double or drop lining of aluminium foil was replaced in favour of the fixed single lining of aluminium foil. [20]

So much did the once beautiful Wolseley fall from grace.

E.T. Renbourn, in the *Journal of Tropical Medicine and Hygiene* writes on the death of the solar topi -

> At the beginning of the Second World War there was a great deal of controversy in official circles as to the virtues of the "Helmet Universal New Pattern" (with aluminium lining), the pith topi ("Bombay Bowler") and a large brimmed felt hat. There was resistance to the general introduction of the latter for English troops, and medical authorities still accepted the idea that the presence of a foil lining gave worthwhile protection...
>
> During the Wavell campaign of 1941 the topi was soon considered an unsuitable form of head-gear and ousted by the Australian slouch-hat (sometimes cocked on the left side) or beret. [21]

According to Brian L. Davis, in Army Council Instruction (ACI) 2661 of December 1942, it was decided that the Wolseley "for wear by British other ranks would be maintained and worn only at certain stations abroad." These stations included; the Sudan, Transjordan and the desert areas of Lebanon. In other areas e.g. Egypt, Palestine, Cyprus and Syria, Wolseleys were worn for use on special duties only.

Davis also states that "helmets at stations abroad that were rendered surplus by these instructions were withdrawn and returned to the RAOC [Royal Army Ordnance Corps] who reconditioned and brought on charge those fit for re-issue or disposed of those considered unserviceable..." [22]

Peter Payne and Jim MacDonald, in *Tanks Again* state that the 2nd Royal Tank Regiment was the last amoured unit to use the Wolseley and this in 1943 in Iraq.[23]

The end is given by John Mollo in the *Formation Sign* magazine when he writes "Pith helmets were still being worn by this Regiment [15th/19th The King's Royal Hussars] in 1949 in Khartoum, apparently the last Regiment to wear them." [24] It is not known whether Mollo was referring to the Wolseley or the Khaki Solar Pith Hat, such is the overlap of terminology used for sun helmets.

The Vocabulary of Clothing and Necessaries of 1949 still listed the Wolseley helmet at a cost of 14 shillings and 6 pence. It is likely that these helmets were reconditioned and issued from RAOC stores. This accords with ACI 2661/1942, mentioned above, which severely restricted the use of Wolseleys and where they were to be used. That ACI also states that -

> **Personnel proceeding from the United Kingdom to tropical or semi-tropical areas for which the helmets, universal, khaki [Wolseley], were previously authorized, will continue to be issued initially with helmets, universal, khaki, before embarkation for use on the voyage. On arrival at the new station, where the helmet, universal, khaki, under this ACI is not worn, it will be retained in possession until personnel become acclimatized or will be replaced by the tropical headgear in use at that station.**

The Wolseley was finally declared obsolete in 1951 in a List of Changes [25], which also stated that all "existing stocks will be returned to RAOC for disposal."

Vale Wolseley.

Some band units, the Royal Marines, some Canadian units and various police, military and para-military forces around the world continue to use the style to this day.

These helmets are usually without puggaree, heavily whitened and sometimes with plastic furniture. A far cry from the elegant Wolseleys of earlier times.

An example of a Khaki Solar Pith Hat which officially replaced the Wolseley in India in 1938. This example has the flash of the Royal Tank Corps Centre and Schools.

The Royal Marines use the Wolseley pattern helmet to this day. It features a cup and ball on a leaf base which was standard for artillery units and derives from that part of the Corps that was the Royal Marine Artillery. This example is dated 1973.

Privates of The Royal Canadian Regiment wearing the Regiment's full dress Wolseley (Courtesy the Department of National Defence).

Chapter 2

British Wolseleys

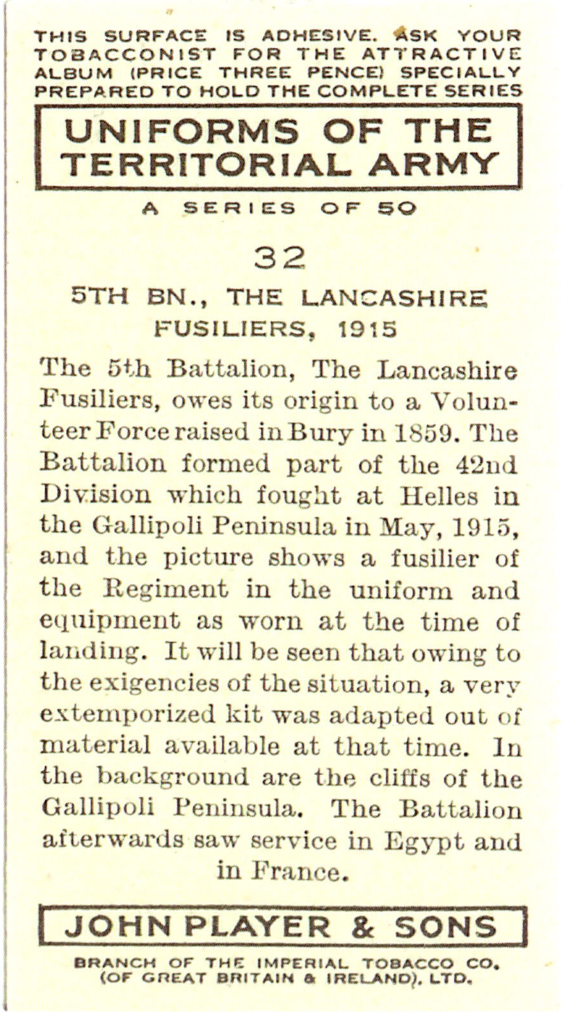
THIS SURFACE IS ADHESIVE. ASK YOUR TOBACCONIST FOR THE ATTRACTIVE ALBUM (PRICE THREE PENCE) SPECIALLY PREPARED TO HOLD THE COMPLETE SERIES

UNIFORMS OF THE TERRITORIAL ARMY

A SERIES OF 50

32

5TH BN., THE LANCASHIRE FUSILIERS, 1915

The 5th Battalion, The Lancashire Fusiliers, owes its origin to a Volunteer Force raised in Bury in 1859. The Battalion formed part of the 42nd Division which fought at Helles in the Gallipoli Peninsula in May, 1915, and the picture shows a fusilier of the Regiment in the uniform and equipment as worn at the time of landing. It will be seen that owing to the exigencies of the situation, a very extemporized kit was adapted out of material available at that time. In the background are the cliffs of the Gallipoli Peninsula. The Battalion afterwards saw service in Egypt and in France.

JOHN PLAYER & SONS

BRANCH OF THE IMPERIAL TOBACCO CO. (OF GREAT BRITAIN & IRELAND), LTD.

A full-dress Wolseley attributed to H.A.O. Hanley DSO, MC of the 2nd Battalion the Middlesex Regiment. It is dated to 1913. Note the high-hook attached to the spike base.

The Middlesex helmet showing the hook under the puggaree for fastening the chinchain when looped up to the hook at the rear of the spike dome base.

The storage/transit tin for the Middlesex helmet opposite. This is a double tin in that it is designed to accommodate two helmets.

A Wolseley to the Army Dental Corps with the flash colours being, from the front, dark blue/red/dark green. The Army Dental Corps was formed in 1921 from the RAMC and became Royal in 1946.

The interior of the Army Dental Corps Wolseley is dated to between 1921 and 1933 shows the maker's label of J. Ellwood & Sons. Sometime in 1933 the company was renamed Ellwood Hats Ltd. Note the unusual ventilator base with seven holes rather than the much more common cartwheel fixing and the corrugated material separating the headband from the shell.

A Royal Artillery helmet of the 66th (South Midland) Field Brigade. This unit existed from 1921 - 1938.

The interior of the 66th Brigade, RA, helmet has handwritten places and dates of where the brigade was stationed. They were; Aldershot, the Military College of Science and Woolwich in 1928, Rawalpindi in 1929 and Hatti in 1930. Other places are mentioned, for example Campbellpore, in modern day Pakistan, but with no date specified.

The sumptuous interior of a rare Wolseley to an Aide-de-Camp which is indicated by the red over white swan feather plume. shown opposite.

The cardboard plume holder which was stored in the bottom of the storage tin.

The ADC's double storage tin which not only accommodates two helmets but also the plume holder.

An extremely rare Full Dress Wolseley to an Aide-de-Camp. This is indicated by the red over white swan feathers in an acanthus leaf base. This helmet is covered in Melton cloth, otherwise known as "doeskin", which is a very fine woollen material.

This photograph shows the Aide-de-Camp Wolseley with the swan feathers removed revealing the acanthus leaf base and plume holder. Note the graduated gilt chinchain and the hook under the puggaree for looping the chinchain up when not in use.

South Lancashire flash (1929-1939) of red cloth embroidered in white with the PoWs' feathers and P.W.V. over South Lancashire (Courtesy of Jon Mills).

The Maltese Cross identifies this regiment as the Wiltshires and the size of the cross dates this photograph to 1924-1937 (Courtesy of Jon Mills).

A straw construction Wolseley attributed to Archibald C. Black of the Royal Army Medical Corps. Paper label shows a date of 1915 and the manufacturer's name E. Day of St. Albans. One of the only two straw Wolseleys known to exist.

Another straw Wolseley being only the second known to exist. This one also made by E. Day of St. Albans and also dated 1915. Attributed to V. E. Morris of the King's Shropshire Light Infantry.

The interior of the straw construction Wolseley. Note the cork spacers between the headband and the helmet shell and the four tabs which are bent up to secure the ventilator cap. The red paper maker's label of E. Day can be clearly seen.

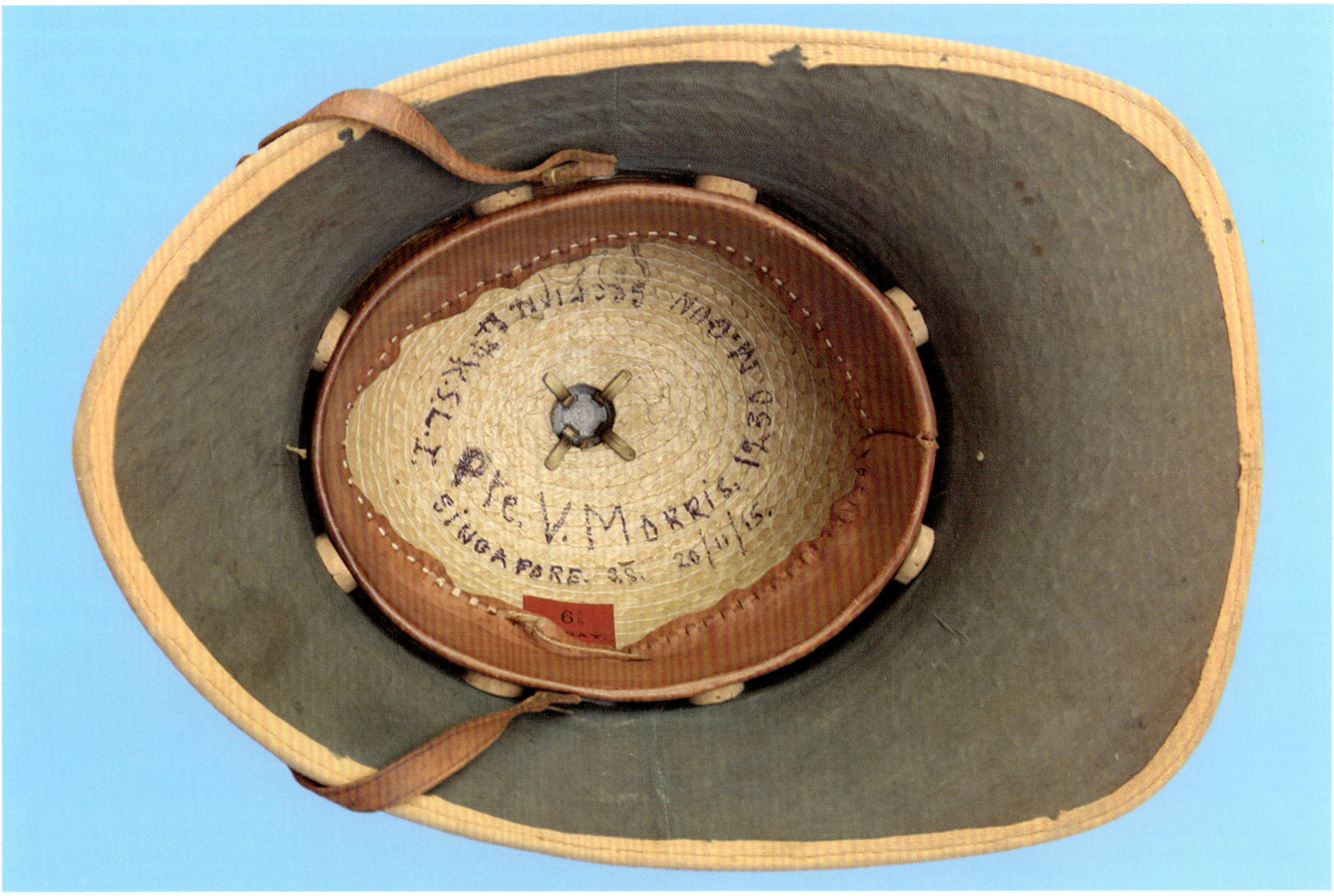

The interior of the King's Shropshire Light Infantry straw Wolseley containing the owner's name, the Regiment's initials (K.S.L.I.) and various other information. The eight cork spacers are clearly shown as are the four tabs bent up to secure the ventilator cap. The red paper label of E. Day is just visible.

Captain K. C. D. Dawson, OBE, Indian Army, 4th Battalion 13th Frontier Force Rifles (Wilde's), ADC to H.E. Field Marshal Lord Birdwood of Anzac and Totnes 1925 - 1930. Captain Dawson is seen wearing the pre 1922 Full Dress uniform of the 57th Wilde's Rifles (FF), Rifles Pattern drab tunic, drab lace and Prussian blue facings. In clear view is his Wolseley Pattern Helmet with spike and base (Courtesy Gordon Byrne).

The Essex Regiment were nicknamed the Pompadours because of the colour of their flash. Originally uniformed with deep crimson facings, which in 1764, were changed to purple. The colour was often called "pompadour" but the reasons for the name of the colour are unclear; it is often said that the shade was Madame de Pompadour's favourite colour.

This Wolseley to the Royal Berkshire Regiment is attributed to Frederick G. Rance who was awarded the Indian General Service medal with Waziristan clasp (1921-1924). The helmet was manufactured by Percy Ayses & Co.

This fine Wolseley features a badge to the Royal Engineers and is circa 1937. The badge has a slider rather than lugs, thereby allowing it to be attached to the helmet without piercing the helmet shell.

The King's Shropshire Light Infantry had a green silk pleat to the top of the puggaree. However, examples are found without such piping.

This rare 1917 dated Wolseley features the red silk piping to the top of the puggaree and indicates the Northumberland Fusiliers. The interior of the Northumberland Fusiliers helmet shows the maker's paper label to E.W. Vero & Co. and is dated 1917.

A 1925 dated helmet to the 8th Hussars which features the Regimental colours in a horsehair hackle of white over red. Note also the wide chinstrap which passes over the top of the helmet, underneath the puggaree and into the interior. The helmet has the usual brass chinstrap hooks even though they are not used.

LIEUT.-GENERAL THE HON. N. G. LYTTELTON

WHEN it was announced that an Army Corps was to be sent to South Africa, and that, wherever possible, regiments were to be brigaded on the good old system of grouping Guards, Fusiliers, and so forth together, a Brigade of Rifles became a foregone conclusion. Everyone, too, with the slightest knowledge of such things, was satisfied and pleased that this Brigade, when formed, should be placed in charge of such an excellent specimen of the Rifleman as Major-General the Hon. N. G. Lyttelton. Judged by actual results, too, the selection has been more than justified, since in all the heavy fighting that took place along the Tugela until Ladysmith was relieved there was no brigade more constantly and more heavily engaged than Lyttelton's. In the history of the war there are few finer episodes than the devoted attempt of this brigade to bring relief to the force at bay on Spion Kop, and throughout this anxious time both it and its commander kept their heads and went on fighting in a manner worthy of the best traditions of the "R.B." and the old Sixtieth.

Major-General The Hon. Neville Gerald Lyttelton, C.B., is the third son of the fourth Baron Lyttelton, and was born in October, 1845. He was educated at Eton, and entered the Rifle Brigade as an Ensign in 1865. From 1869 to 1873 he served as Aide-de-Camp to Lord Spencer during the latter's term as Lord Lieutenant of Ireland, and four years later saw service in the Jowaki Expedition of 1877. After a short spell at the War Office as Private Secretary to the Secretary of State, he accompanied the Egyptian Expedition of 1882 as A.D.C. to the Chief of the Staff, and was present at the battle of Tel-el-Kebir. For his services in this campaign he received a brevet lieutenant-colonelcy.

From 1883 to 1885 Colonel Lyttelton was Military Secretary to Sir John Adye, Governor of Gibraltar, and from 1885 to 1890 he acted in a similar capacity on the Staff of Lord Reay, Governor of Bombay. In 1892 he became a substantive lieutenant-colonel, and commanded the 2nd Battalion Rifle Brigade at Dublin until 1894. He relinquished his command to go to the War Office as Assistant Adjutant-General, being subsequently transferred to the Military Secretary's Department in 1898. In the latter year he was, with the late Major-General Wauchope, selected for the command of a British brigade in the final advance on Khartoum. The manner in which he carried out this duty was recognised by special promotion to the rank of Major-General, and in 1899, the command of an Infantry brigade at Aldershot falling vacant, he obtained that coveted billet, thereby rendering his selection for South Africa doubly certain. At the close of the war General Lyttelton will presumably return to a post for which, apart from his ability, smartness, and varied regimental experience, he will have further qualified by the tenure of two important brigade commands on active service.

[Since the above was written, General Lyttelton has been appointed to the command of the 4th Division, which forms part of the Field Force in Natal.]

From a Photograph by *C. Knight.*

LIEUTENANT-GENERAL THE HON. N. G. LYTTELTON, C.B.

COMMANDING FOURTH BRIGADE IN SOUTH AFRICA.

General Lyttelton as a Staff Officer which is indicated by his collar gorgets. Note the piping to his helmet puggaree which also indicates a Staff Officer (Collection of Stuart Bates).

A Sherwood Foresters helmet with the distinctive green cloth band around and under the top of the puggaree.

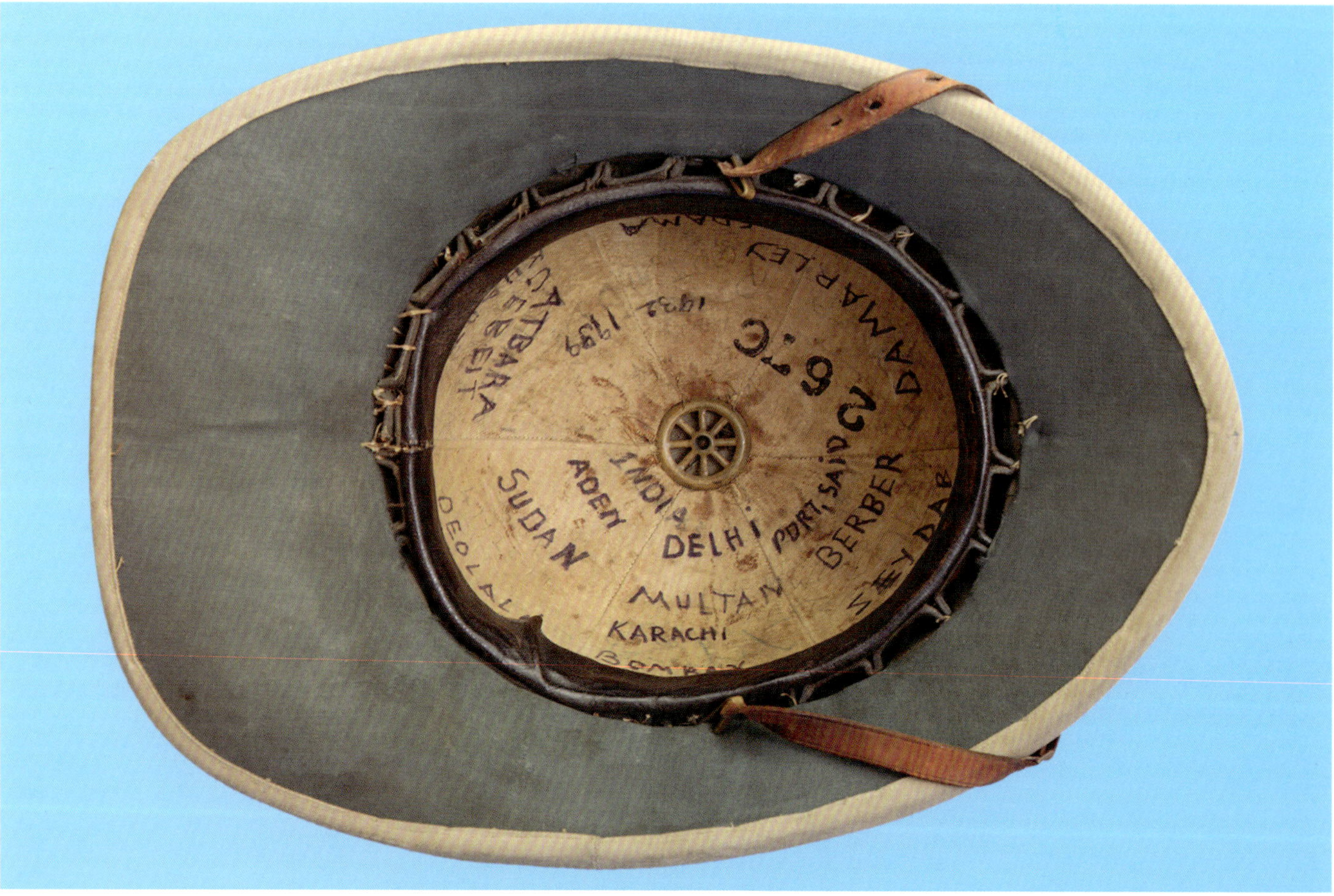

The interior of the Sherwood Foresters' helmet where the owner has written every station at which he served in addition to the dates 1932-1939. It was unusual for a cork Wolseley to last that length of service, but was probably supplemented by a Cawnpore or Khaki Solar Pith Helmet.

This helmet features the flash of the $14^{th}/20^{th}$ Hussars who served in Egypt 1931 and India 1933-1944. This regiment was created in 1922 by the amalgamation of the 14th King's Hussars and the 20th Hussars.

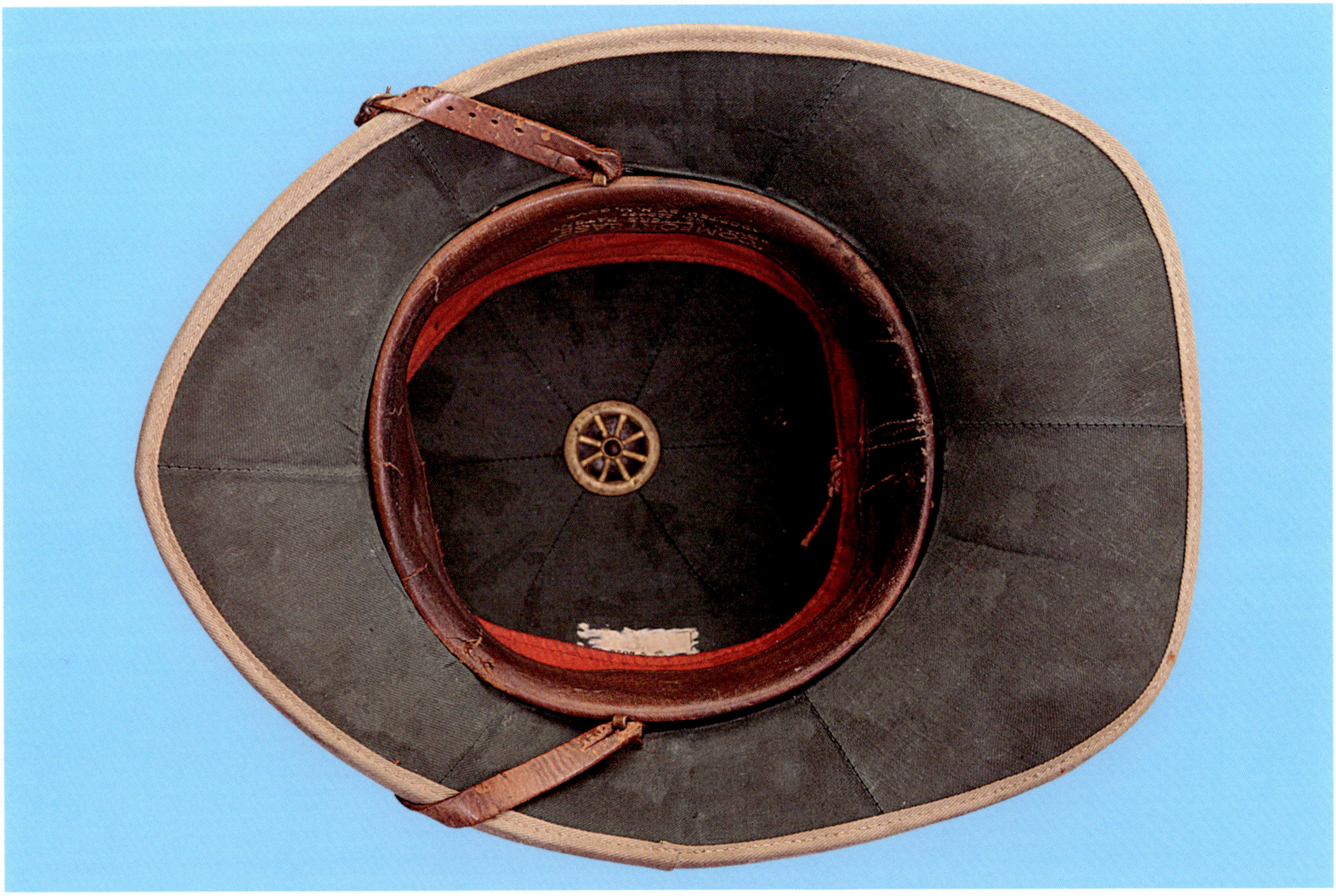

The interior of the $14^{th}/20^{th}$ Hussars showing the paper label of the manufacturer, Hobson & Sons. The leather headband is a later addition. It is a Vero's detachable headband but is glued directly to the helmet shell either as a "field-repair" or to improve the helmet's saleability. *Caveat emptor.*

The Middlesex helmet with cotton cover which was issued to Other Ranks. Officers often had storage/transit tins to protect their private purchase helmets.

Another view of the cover for Wolseley helmets issued to Other Ranks.

A Middlesex Regiment helmet showing not only the yellow piping to the puggaree but a flash with the Middlesex badge. Manufactured by Percy Ayses, London.

Left is a soldier of the King's (Lancaster) Regiment and on the right a signaller of The Royal Engineers (Signals). Note the crossed flags badge (Courtesy of Jon Mills).

Soldiers of the 5th Battalion East Surrey Regiment (Courtesy of Jon Mills).

This helmet is attributed to the 2nd Earl of Cromer who gained the rank of 2nd Lieutenant in the Grenadier Guards in WWI. He held the office of ADC to the Viceroy of India 1915-1916 and was Chief of Staff to the Duke of Connaught 1920-1921 in India.

A front shot of the Earl of Cromer's helmet. Unfortunately the Grenadier Guards puggaree badge is missing.

The storage/transit tin of the Earl of Cromer's Wolseley. This is a double tin in that it can accommodate two helmets.

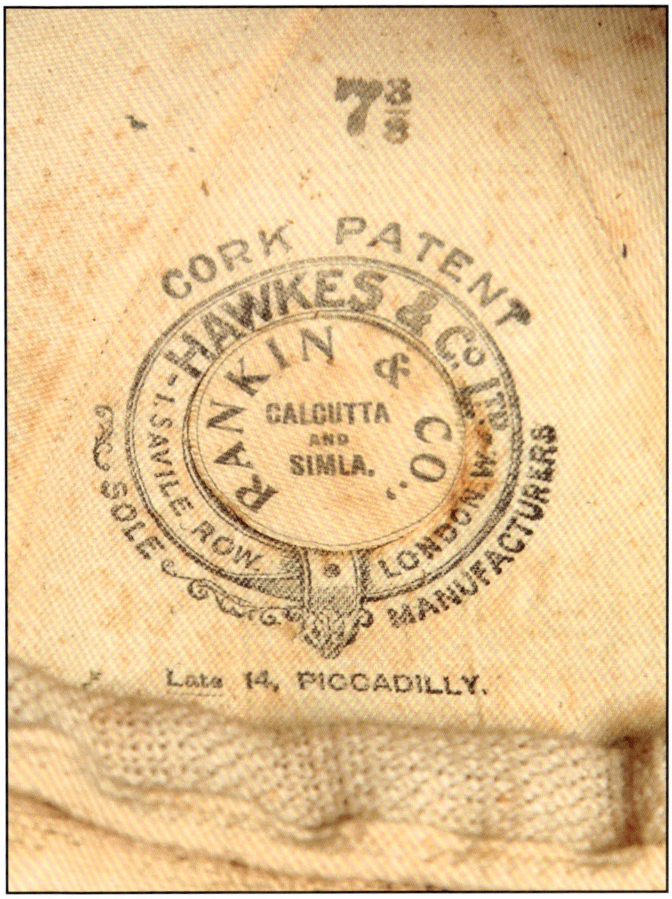

The interior of the Earl of Cromer's Wolseley showing Hawkes manufacture and retailed by Rankin & Co. of Calcutta and Simla. Note the cotton mesh affixed to the leather headband instead of the more usually seen red silk on officers' private purchase helmets.

1/5th Battalion, The Gloucestershire Regiment in Italy, July 1918. They are wearing a diamond shaped flash, probably red, with the regimental badge of the Sphinx affixed to it (Courtesy Soldiers of Gloucestershire Museum).

A Scots Guard's helmet with a flash to both the right and left hand side. This example also features a regimental badge which perforates the shell.

The left hand side of the Scots Guards helmet displaying the red/white/black diced flash.

A World War II Royal Air Force Wolseley.

This flash indicates the 7th Queen's Own Hussars. The colours are yellow on a dark blue background, however the yellow has faded to almost white.

A wonderful tinted postcard of a soldier of the The Queen's Royal Regiment (West Surrey). Note the flash extends well past the puggaree. The collar badges indicate that this photograph was taken in the early to mid 1920s as a new style badge was authorised in 1924.

This helmet displays the 3rd style flash of the famous 7th Armoured Division of the 8th Army and is constructed from felt rather than the usual cork. The tin or aluminium foil to the interior is shown below.

Tin or aluminium foil was used at various times throughout the life of the Wolseley but its effectiveness as heat protection is debatable. Leather strips are stitched to the headband and fit over metal prongs riveted through the shell to provide ventilation. Note also the four bent up tabs which secure the ventilator cap. These were used because of the felt construction of the helmet.

A splendid photograph showing four soldiers in tropical dress, probably from an artillery unit which is indicated by the badge on the helmet of the soldier extreme left. The "horse bit" insignia on the seated soldier's right sleeve indicates a saddler and the shoulder titles could very well be the Honourable Artillery Company. The men wear the 1903 bandolier which was replaced in 1908 but mainly taken up by the infantry. The older bandoliers were used for many years by other units of the British Army.

A Wolseley to the Royal Corps of Signals circa 1934. The flash colours are light blue/dark blue/green although the light blue has faded over time. This style of flash was authorised in 1934 and replaced in 1937 by piping to the top of the puggaree in the Corps colours with light blue to the top.

Another example of a Wolseley to the Royal Corps of Signals with this one showing the flash having been applied back-to-front.

An unadorned Wolseley with a lovely 9 pleat puggaree, retailed in Nairobi, Kenya by Cearn & Co.

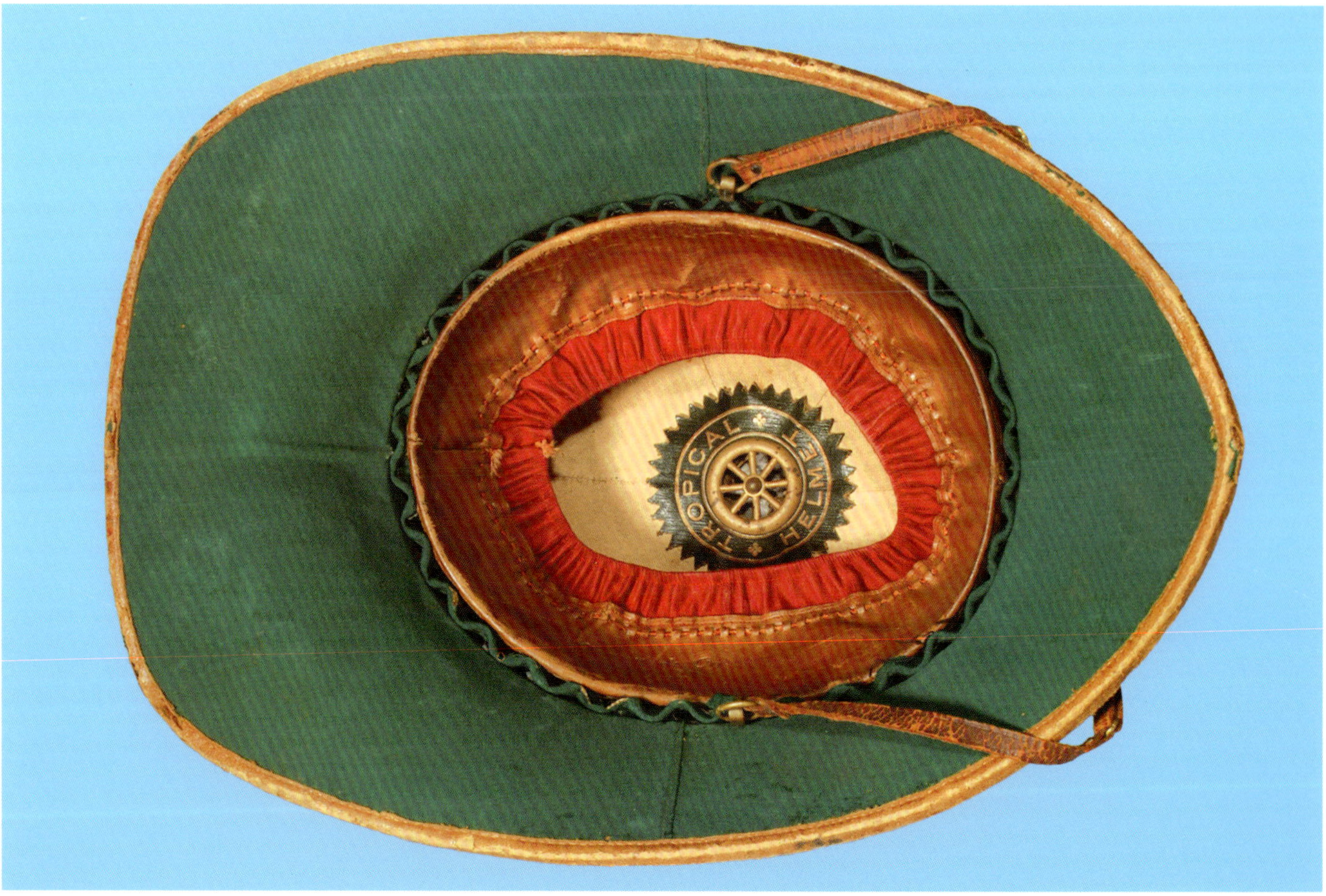

The interior of the Nairobi Wolseley showing the red silk sweatband, which indicates an officer's private purchase helmet. Note the rings to the ends of the chinstrap rather than the much more common cuts into the chinstrap ends which looped over the attaching hooks. This example also features the corrugation between the shell and the headband.

The front view of the Nairobi helmet.

Stamped into the leather headband of the Nairobi helmet is the retailer's name - Cearn & Co. of Nairobi, Kenya.

A splendid study of a Lancashire Fusilier showing his Wolseley helmet complete with flash and primrose hackle (Courtesy of Jon Mills).

A Wolseley bearing the flash of the famous Lancashire Fusiliers who fought in the Gallipoli Campaign of 1915.

The yellow and blue piping to this helmet identify the regiment as the East Kent (Buffs).

A Wolseley to the Royal Navy with the distinctive blue pleat to the top of the puggaree. The Royal Navy adopted the Wolseley helmet in 1906 and discontinued its use in 1949. [26]

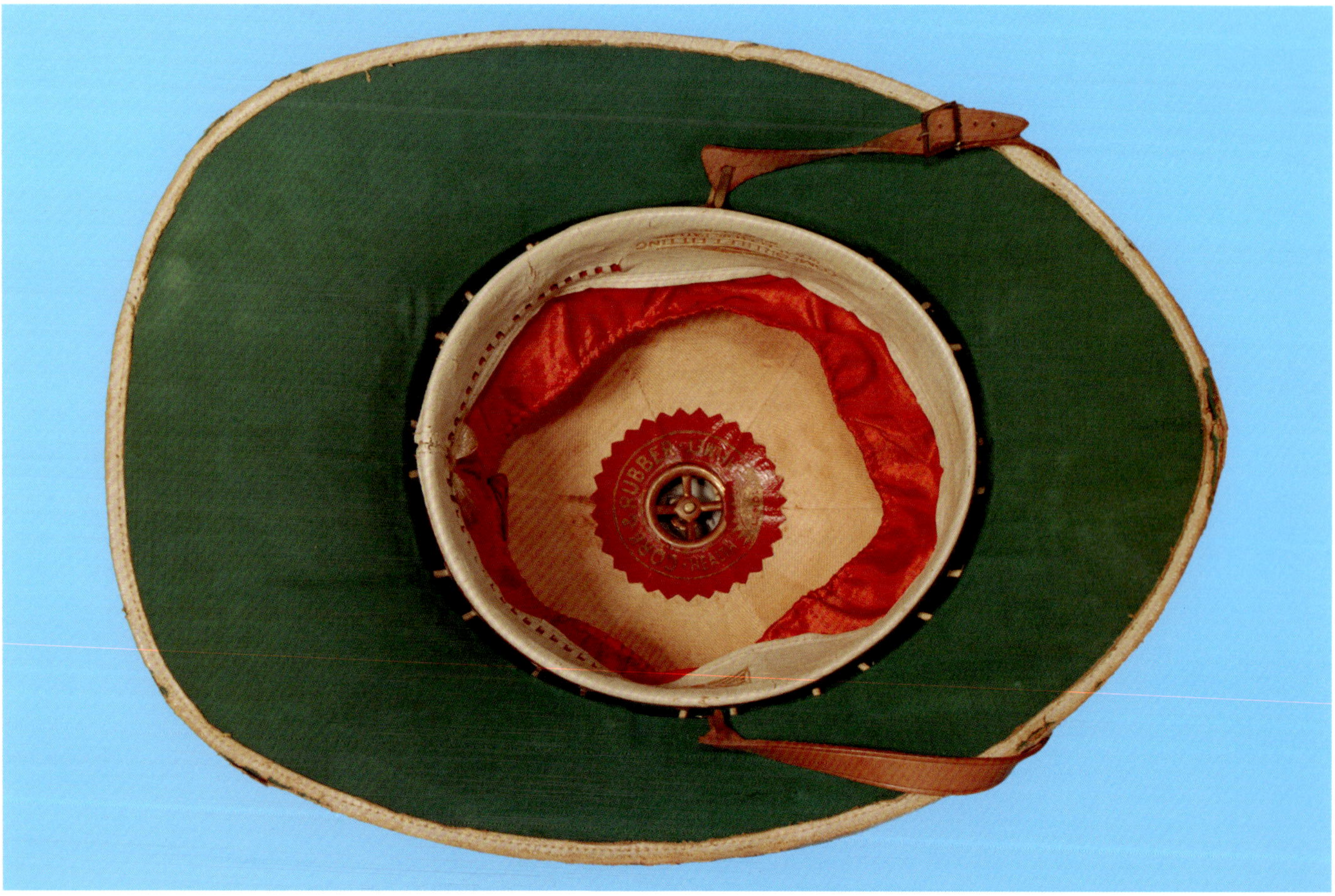

This Royal Navy Wolseley utilises the Charles Owen & Co. system of providing an air-space between the helmet shell and the headband. This patent was granted in 1923.

The headband stamp which shows the patent information for an adjustable headband granted to Charles Owen & Co. in 1923.

The Royal Navy helmet also has this unusual image of the Union Flag stamped into the leather headband.

This proud soldier belongs to the Duke of Wellington's Regiment (West Riding) and shows the strip of scarlet cloth to the top of the puggaree. The regimental cap badge affixed to a red cloth patch dates this photo to 1926 - 1929 and is possibly the 2nd Battalion. He wears a machine gun badge above a good conduct chevron on his left sleeve (Courtesy of Jon Mills).

A Wolseley to the Duke of Wellington's Regiment. The flash is post 1929 and appears in photographs of the 1st Battalion in Malta in 1937 (Courtesy of Jon Mills).

An Other Rank's Wolseley circa 1933-1942. The lack of a puggaree indicates that this helmet was probably unissued or manufactured after the puggaree was dispensed with. The flipped headband is a mystery as these were normally a straight piece of cloth to hide the mechanics of fixing the internal headband and chinstrap loops (Courtesy of Soldiers of Gloucestershire Museum).

In 1917 the Tank Corps was formed from the Heavy Branch of the Machine Gun Corps and in 1923 became the Royal Tank Corps. It became the Royal Tank Regiment in 1939. This photo shows three members of the 41st RTR in Egypt 1941 (Courtesy of Jim MacDonald).

A Wolseley flash to the 5th Armoured Car Company of the Royal Tank Corps. This unit was stationed in China 1927-1929 and Egypt 1929-1933 (Courtesy of Jim MacDonald).

A close-up of a puggaree badge worn on the Wolseley helmet. Note that this example is *not* of the slider type whereas the one shown opposite is (Courtesy of Jim MacDonald).

A fine Wolseley to the Royal Tank Regiment. The colours of brown/red/green signify the unofficial motto "From Mud, Through Blood to the Green Fields Beyond." Wolseleys were worn from the 1920s to the mid 1940s by armoured units and this example is dated 1940 (Courtesy of Peter Payne).

The Royal Tank Regiment puggaree badge is clearly seen in this front shot of the Royal Tank Regiment Wolseley (Courtesy of Peter Payne).

This example has a plain 10 pleat puggaree but with the addition of a Machine Gun Corps puggaree slider badge. The helmet is dated 1915.

Corporal Harold Bates, RASC, during training in Durban, South Africa, before deployment to the Western Desert. He is wearing a felt Wolseley.

A soldier of the Royal West Kent Regiment. His Wolseley has the regimental patch of the White Horse of Kent over the motto *INVICTA* which means "Unconquered".

This Wolseley is attributed to Captain A.K. Phillips of the 1st Battalion, West Yorkshire Regiment (Prince of Wales's Own). It has the cloth patch authorised in the 1929 Clothing Regulations of the White Horse of Hanover over the motto *Nec Aspera Terrent* **which translates as "And They Fear Not Hardship" (Courtesy of York Museums Trust /York Castle Museum).**

A donkey in full marching order. He appears to be wearing a Sherwood Forester's Wolseley and a side (rump) cap of the Royal Inniskilling Fusiliers (Photo courtesy Peter Payne).

A full dress white Wolseley with an unusual vertical pleated flash to which was affixed another flash, now missing. Note the hook under the puggaree for looping up the chin chain, actually obscured by the chinchain itself in this photo (Courtesy of York Museums Trust /York Castle Museum).

The high-hook is missing on this white full dress helmet and therefore the chinchain has been tucked into the puggaree (Courtesy of York Museums Trust /York Castle Museum).

A radio party in the field, Quetta, India, 1932.

The reverse of the radio party photo.

The Somerset Light Infantry (Prince Albert's Own) wore a dark green patch with the Regimental badge embroidered on it in "old gold" (Courtesy of Jon Mills).

This Wolseley bears the post-war Territorial Army arm badge worn by the RA's 88 Army Group Royal Artillery (AGRA) between 1948 and 1956. As it was an arm badge it came in facing pairs and the one shown here is incorrect for the side of the helmet on which it is affixed. This arrangement indicates a "made-up" helmet to improve saleability. *Caveat emptor.*

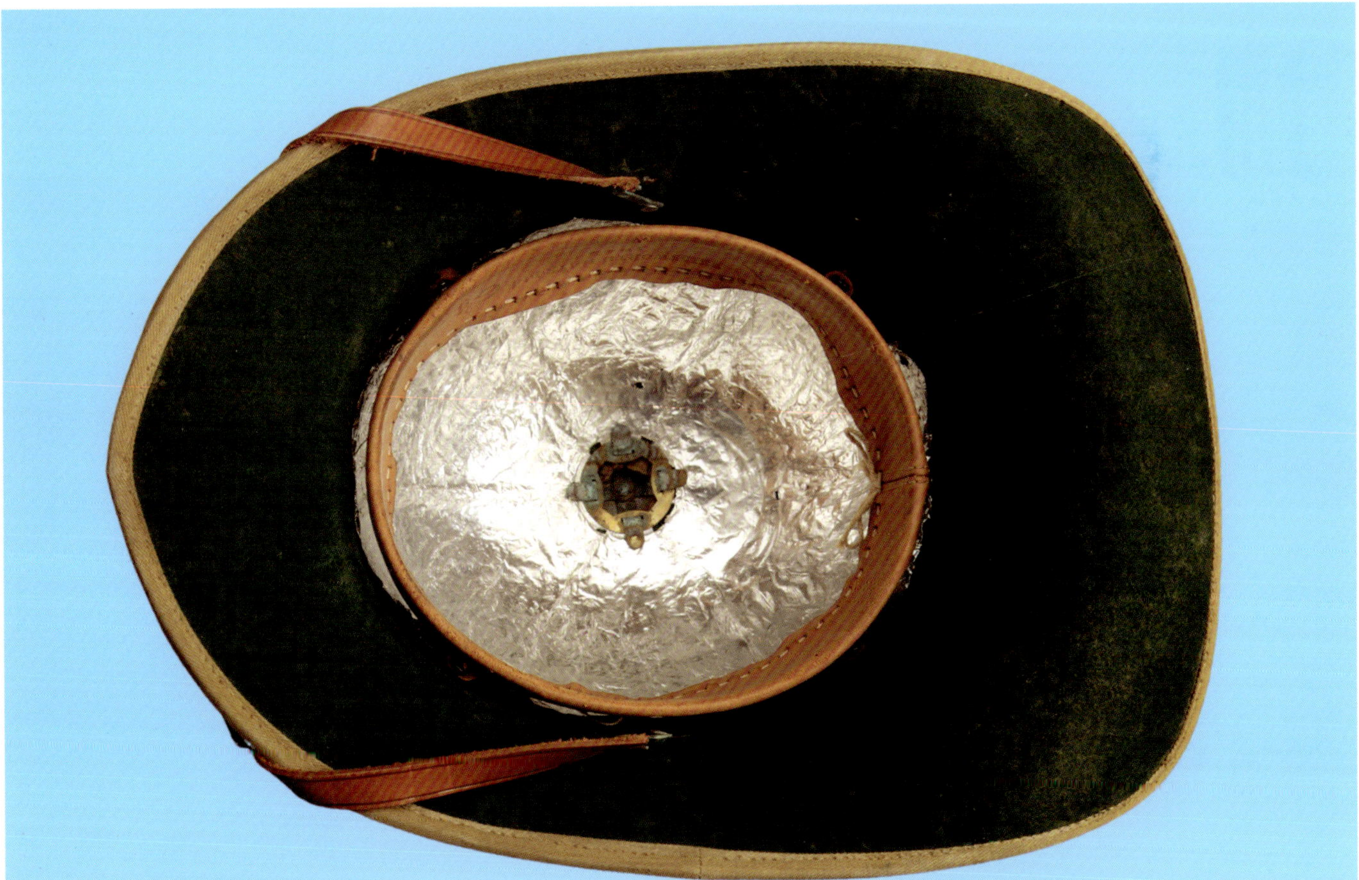

The interior of the "RA's 88 Army Group Royal Artillery" Wolseley showing the usual foil lining, detachable headband and felt construction.

The interior of the "RA's 88 AGRA" helmet ventilator cap from the interior. Note the plate used to strengthen the four tabs from the ventilator cap and the rivet fixing the crosspiece to that ventilator cap.

The maker's label of the "RA's 88 AGRA" helmet. Failsworth Hats Ltd were founded in 1903 in Manchester and are in existence today.

An officer, wearing a Wolseley, inspecting the 2nd Battalion RoyalTank Corps, India, in the late 1930s (Courtesy Peter Payne).

Garrison police in Darjeeling 1924. The helmets with the dark vertical flash on a light (yellow?) background would indicate the Norfolk Regiment and the helmets with the dark rectangular flash are the 2nd Battalion the Durham Light Infantry (Courtesy of Jon Mills).

A soldier of the Worcestershire Regiment showing the green painted ventilator cap on his Wolseley helmet which was unique to this regiment. However, the cap was reported to cause problems of excessive heat when exposed to the sun.

Chapter 3
Experimental Wolseleys And Others

The continual change in British War Material is proof enough of the constant search for better design and function - showing by illustration and sometimes by example the ongoing improvements and developments taking place behind the scenes of war.

The primary tropical headdress of the second half of the 19th century, the Foreign Service Helmet was also subject to change throughout its long life. Its major function had been to provide protection from the sun in harsh desert and tropical regions, and while it was a pattern that was soon copied and adopted by other nations its design was constantly being reviewed.

From its beginnings in the 1840s, sun helmet design not only focused on protection from the sun, but also on the best means of ventilating the interior of the helmet, giving air flow and a cooling effect when most needed.

Thus the search for a new design often required the manufacture of alternative patterns. These were then trialled to evaluate their protective qualities, and the function and durability of the materials from which the item was made. These items are possibly best described as "experimental."

As a result they were produced in very limited numbers, and those experimental helmets that failed the trials were quite often lost, destroyed or even had their components recycled. Some were obviously taken by or sold to soldiers participating in the trials.

For this reason, these experimental patterns are highly desirable, not only to the student and collector of military headdress, but as a tangible historical record of proposed items of equipment, whether practical or not, as these show the innovation and design as it was in past days of the Empire.

The Royal Army Ordnance Depot, Branston, donated the surviving prototypes described in this chapter to the York Castle Museum in the 1950s and they have only recently been brought into the light by Keith Matthews, Curator of Military History, York Museums Trust (York Castle Museum).

The Visor Experimental Wolseley

One such experimental Wolseley illustrates, in graphic manner, an attempt which no doubt places function ahead of the aesthetic quality of the helmet.

Keith Matthews describes the helmet as having 17 holes of 11mms (5/16ths of an inch) diameter crudely drilled through the front of the helmet over which is glued a cloth mesh. This mesh was meant to keep insects and other foreign objects from entering the helmet, and the holes to allow greater and improved airflow.

This photo of the experimental helmet shows the second brim or visor attached by a cloth band around the helmet and whose function is to protect the ventilation holes (Courtesy of York Museums Trust /York Castle Museum).

A front view of the experimental Wolseley helmet showing the protective second brim or visor (Courtesy of York Museums Trust /York Castle Museum).

A closeup view of the seventeen mesh covered ventilation holes drilled through the front of the experimental helmet (Courtesy of York Museums Trust /York Castle Museum).

A view of the dried glue and cloth remnants around the brim of the helmet which probably formed the base of an insect veil (Courtesy of York Museums Trust /York Castle Museum).

An additional brim or visor was attached to the helmet by a cloth band around the circumference of the helmet to provide protection to the ventilation holes from the sun and rain. This brim or visor arrangement is of superior quality to the other modifications.

Traces of a fine fabric remain glued to the under side of the main helmet brim, which suggests that this was an additional insect curtain for tropical/desert conditions. It may have had a drawstring not only to stop insects from entering from below but also to keep the veil in place when it was rolled up over the top of the brim. However, this must remain speculation until additional information comes to light.

It is interesting to note that there are four additional dollops of glue inboard of the glue line at the rear of the helmet some of which retain traces of a very thin coarsely woven white cotton fabric. One suggestion is that the fabric was folded back onto the extra glue to give added strength when the helmet was being donned, with the veil already rolled down, and was pulled over the head.

Alternatively, the material may have originated at the inboard glue line and then extended from there around the circumference of the brim in a spiral manner. The angle of the remaining cloth at the first point on the circumference seems to support this view.

Matthews says that the material used for this veil is of such a light weight that any other form of fixing it to the helmet, rather than gluing, would have been impractical. This suggests that this veil was an afterthought and never pursued past the original prototype.

The leather headband is stamped with "Vero's Detachable & Self-Conforming Headband. Royal Letters Patent No. 228467". This patent was granted in 1925.

There is also a stamp to the top of the crown giving a patent date of 7th September 1933 for the foil lining, and the patent number of 397985 which was granted in 1933 to Guy Pascoe Crowden. This stamp suggests that the foil liner made the helmet 10-15 degrees Farenheit cooler and is "Recommended by the Tropical Research

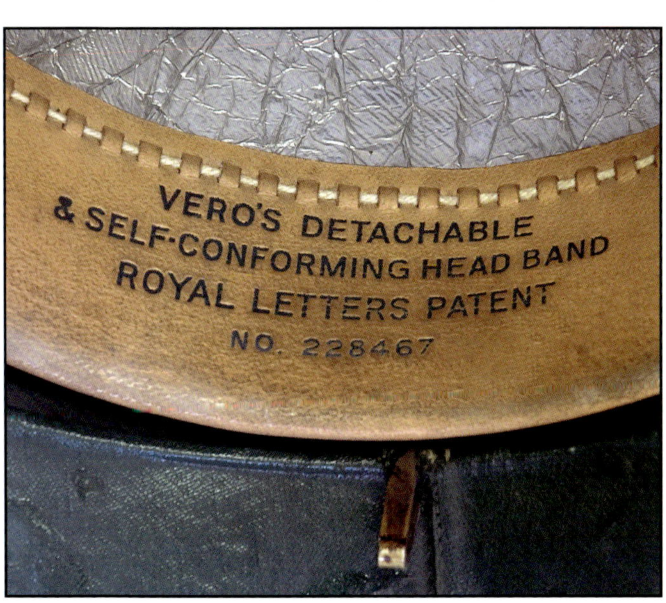

The Vero's stamp for the headband patent of 1925 (Courtesy of York Museums Trust /York Castle Museum).

The stamp showing details of the 1933 patent for the foil lining (Courtesy of York Museums Trust /York Castle Museum).

Department." This latter patent then dates the helmet to 1933-1942.

This remarkable experimental Wolseley illustrates both quality and crude workmanship, further suggesting that this may have been a "one off" test subject. However, no additional information is yet known about this helmet.

The Dark Blue Wolseleys

These, otherwise quite standard Wolseleys are a mystery being covered with a dark blue woollen cloth and with woollen puggarees of various colours The dark blue colour is obviously unsuited to a hot climate.

Each helmet is fitted with a leather strip just under the puggaree on the left hand side but still visible. This was presumably to allow for the attachment of a plume or hackle.

All are fitted with Vero's Detachable headband and a drop foil lining and two have an E.W. Vero paper maker's label visible and dated 1938. It is therefore safe to assume that these helmets were all made by E.W. Vero & Co. in 1938.

Other attachments are as follows -

Yellow puggaree - brown leather chinstrap, blackened chinchain, hook under puggaree on the left hand side. High-hook between first and second pleat of puggaree.

Red Puggaree - brass chinchain, hook under puggaree on the left hand side. High-hook between first and second pleat of puggaree.

White Puggaree - black leather chinstrap, hook under puggaree on the left hand side.

Black Puggaree - brown leather chinstrap, no hook under puggaree.

The four dark blue Wolseleys. Note the leather strip under the puggaree on the black puggaree version (Courtesy of York Museums Trust /York Castle Museum).

The chinchain hook under the puggaree is clearly shown here with a blackened bronze or brass chinchain attached. Note also the leather strip stitched onto the shell to accommodate a plume of hackle (Courtesy of York Museums Trust /York Castle Museum).

The hook under the puggaree was to accommodate a chinchain looped up to the right hand side when not worn under the chin. The black puggaree version does not have this hook but it is presumed that this fitting has come adrift at some time and been lost.

What is also interesting about these helmets is that the high-hook is embedded between the first and second fold of the puggaree. The normal position of the high-hook was to the top rear of the helmet crown or fixed to the base of the spike if fitted.

Black leather chinstraps and blackened chinchains usually indicate Rifle regiments but no assumptions can be made about these helmets on that basis.

The high-hook is clearly seen here between the first and second pleat of the puggaree (Courtesy of York Museums Trust /York Castle Museum).

Four Seam Wolseley

This interesting variation of the Wolseley was produced in 1941 and 1942 but in what numbers it is difficult to ascertain. It is unusual in that it has only four seams, positioned north, south, east and west, rather than the six seams as specified in the regulations. There are only three wartime examples currently known.

What is also interesting is that, even though this helmet is made of cork, it has a faux ventilator cap i.e. one that provides no air flow into or out of the helmet. In fact this ventilator cap is simply sewn to the top of the helmet, although holes have been, rather crudely, made through the crown shell to provide some basic ventilation. The other examples included in this book, of Canadian and Australian manufacture, have normal ventilator caps.

The helmet has a distinctly rounded peak which differs from the usual more pointed specimens. The two Australian post-World War II examples and the 1942 Canadian example, described in their relevant chapters, also feature the four seams and the style characteristics

A Wolseley which has only four seams, a faux ventilator and no puggaree. This one is dated 1941.

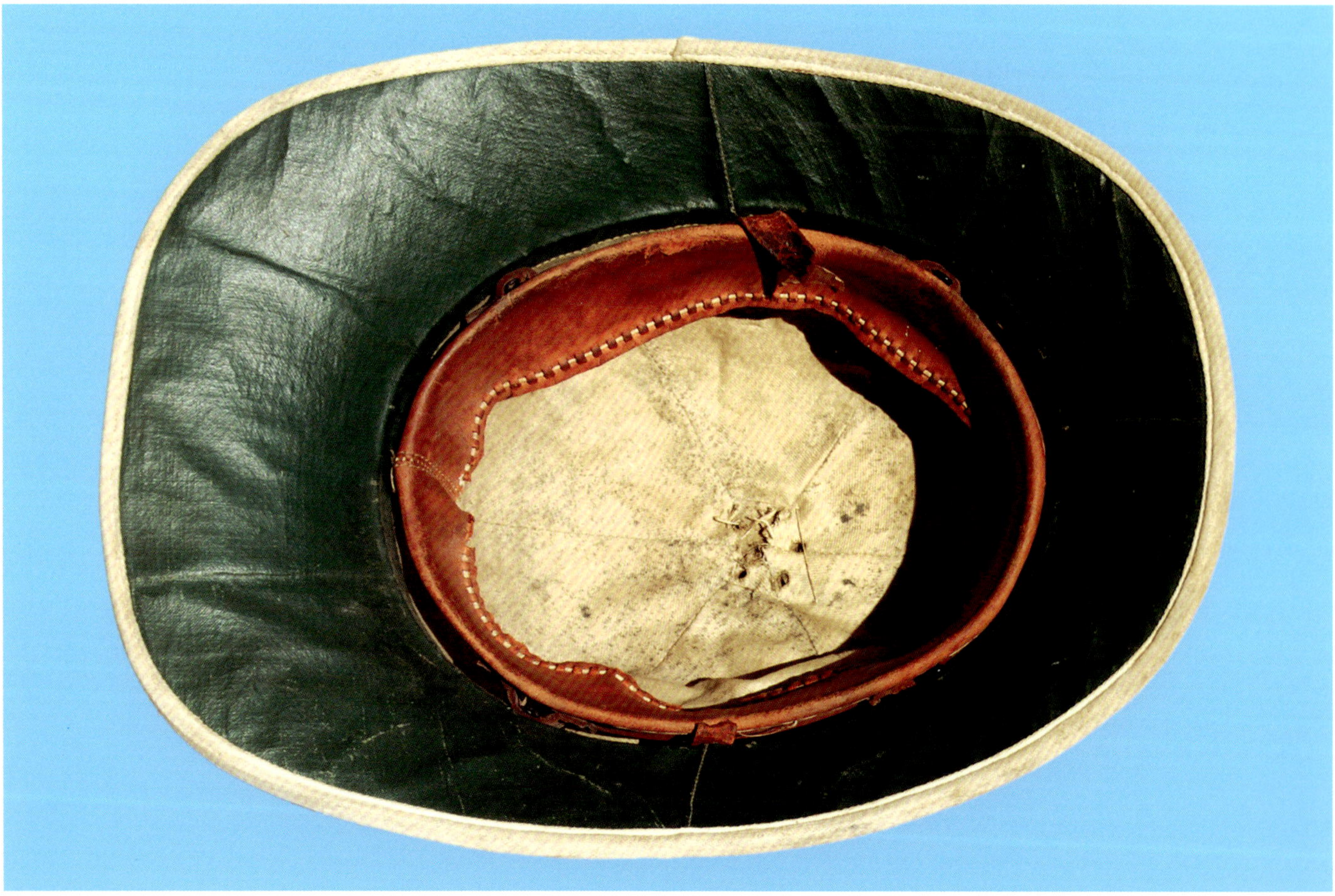

The inside of the 1941 dated four seam Wolseley. Note the holes crudely punched into the crown shell to allow some ventilation from the, otherwise, faux ventilator cap.

The maker's stamp of Helmets Ltd., Wheathampstead, Hertfordshire. Wheathampstead is near St Albans which was a major hat/helmet manufacturing town. The St Albans firm, E. Day, makers of straw helmets, moved all its operations to Wheathampstead as Helmets Ltd. circa 1917.

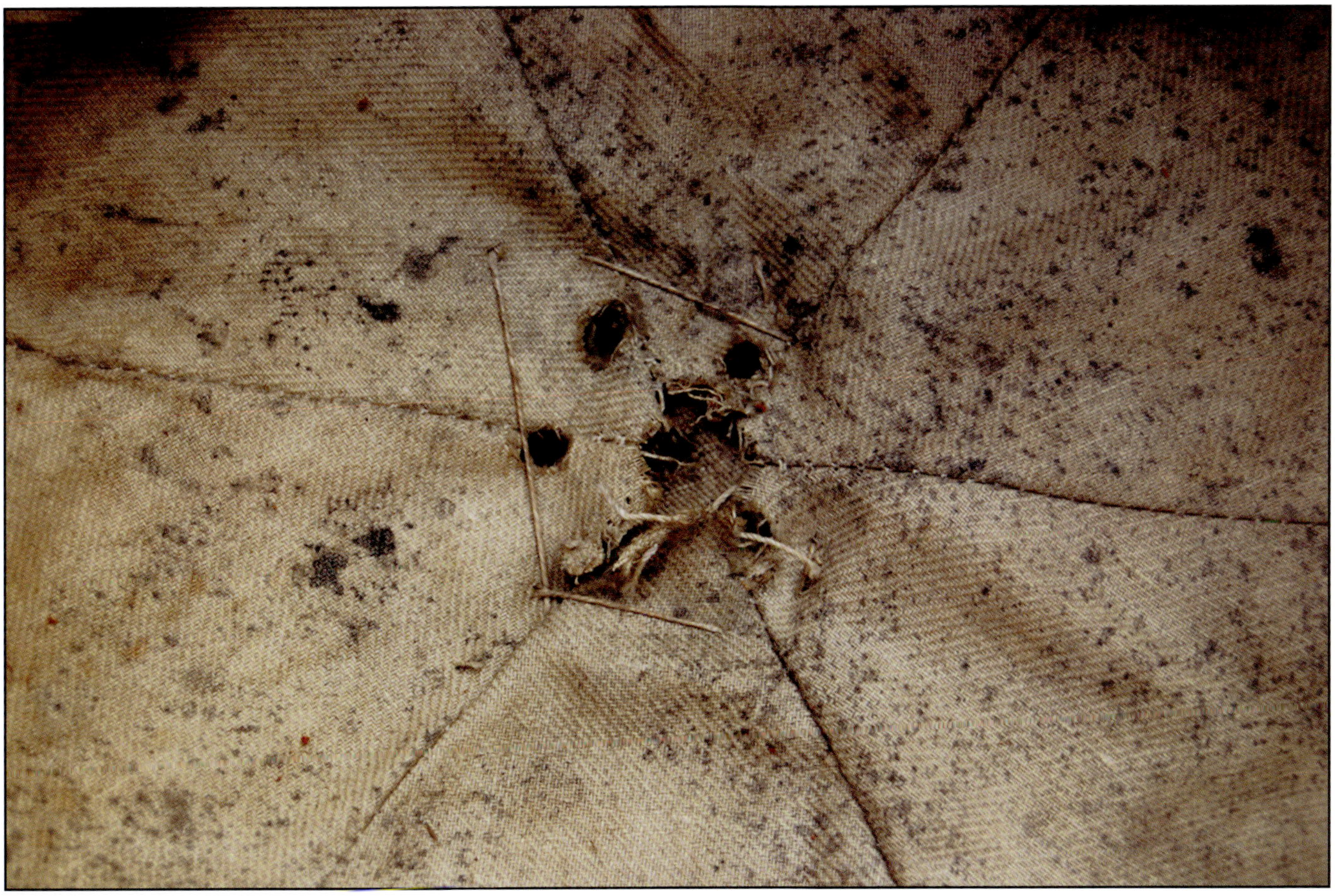

The stitching, within the Wolseley four seamer, securing the ventilator cap to the helmet is clearly shown here as are the holes punched through the shell to provide some ventilation.

This photo shows the liner having been sewn first and then glued to the cork. No signs of glue are present on the cork itself so it would seem that the drill cotton - both exterior and interior - provided the strength and stability of the helmet.

of this helmet.

These helmets seem to have been used by naval and air forces.

Chapter 4
Australian Wolseleys

The Wolseley was never a general issue helmet for the Australian Forces but some Corps/departments did adopt it. Generally speaking, the slouch hat or steel helmet were the preferred headgear for the Australian Forces. Officers, however, could purchase Wolseley helmets privately.

The Australian Intelligence Corps were authorised to wear the Wolseley by order MO 336/1908. This Wolseley was specified as having a puggaree of seven pleats with the centre pleat being pale blue. A small corps badge was worn to the front.

During the First World War the British Army supplied Wolseleys to Australian Forces for service in Gallipoli and the Middle East but the uptake does not seem to have been great. Elements of the Australian Artillery wore the Wolseley in Egypt from 1915 but it was by no means a general issue.

In the Second World War Australian-made Wolseleys were worn by the Royal Australian Air Force, the Royal Australian Navy and various other units. The Royal Australian Navy also wore Wolseleys well into the post World War II period.

A full dress Wolseley to the Australian Infantry with a badge surmounted by a Queen Elizabeth crown which dates this helmet from 1953. Manufactured by Hobson & Sons.

A very interesting example to Captain A.L. Fitzpatrick, 1st Light Horse, AIF. It shows shrapnel or bullet damage sustained during the battle of Romani, 4th August 1916. Captain Fitzpatrick was wounded in the head and neck. He was discharged as medically unfit in 1917 (Courtesy of the Australian War Memorial, negative number RELAWM09710).

A very rare Wolseley to the Australian Engineers dated 1914 and manufactured by J. Hobson & Sons. The badge has two lugs which perforate the shell and a cotter pin passing through them to secure the badge.

Taken in Egypt 1915 this photograph shows five members of the AIF in tropical kit wearing the Wolseley helmet or the Khaki Solar Pith Hat. The fact of their holding canes and posing in front of a canvas backdrop indicates that they are performing in a concert (Courtesy of the Australian War Memorial, negative number P02406_003).

A Wolseley to Private Reginald Harry Quarmby, 17 Battalion AIF and circa 1915. He enlisted in October 1915 and returned to Australia in April 1916. Note the hand-drawn Rising Sun and the word "ANZAC". This helmet was issued in Egypt (Courtesy of the Australian War Memorial, negative number REL27153).

A Wolseley to the Royal Australian Navy with a blue painted metal badge. Note that this helmet follows the World War II four panel pattern, despite the probability that it was made well after the war. This helmet was manufactured by E.M. Belton & Co, Melbourne Australia

A white Wolseley and calico drawstring bag attributed to T.J. O'Connor, RAN, who served at the gunnery school Flinders Naval Depot, Victoria. Manufactured by Belton Ltd, Melbourne. This helmet also has only four seams rather than the usual six (Courtesy of the Australian War Memorial, negative number REL20532).

This Wolseley is to the Royal Australian Airforce and has the name Flight Sergeant Thompson written to the interior. It has a maker's stamp of a Melbourne manufacturer which is unfortunately illegible. However, "Made entirely in Melbourne" is clearly visible. Note the flash is affixed to the right hand side.

A rifle range at RAF Kota Bharu, Malaya in 1941. Note the mixture of Wolseley helmets and Khaki Solar Pith Hats (Courtesy of the Australian War Memorial, negative number P02266_016).

Chapter 5

Canadian Wolseleys

The Wolseley Helmet was introduced into Canadian Service on 9 July 1910, by Militia Order 260, as an advance notification of the intent to formally adopt the helmet into general use within the year. In 1911 the following was published as Militia Order No. 490.

> **"Wolseley pattern helmets will now be issued to the Permanent Force in exchange for the old pattern white helmet. Officers Commanding units should indent for them in the usual manner, and, on their receipt, should return the old pattern helmets to Ordnance charge. The metal fittings and puggarees now in charge of units will be retained for use on the Wolseley helmet and, therefore, will not be replaced."**

Although a sun helmet such as the Wolseley may appear to be an incongruous choice for a country best known for its cold winter climate, Canada's summers are both sunny and hot and the Wolseley was a welcome replacement to the white "universal pattern helmet - the Canadian term for the British Foreign Service Helmet.

In keeping with British practice the white Wolseley became the de facto full dress headdress for any unit which did not already lay claim to specific full dress headdress - such as the Guards' bearskin cap, the Busby, or Dragoon helmet. Although there was a desire to move away from the Wolseley in the immediate pre-Second World War years, British intransigence delayed any change and the Wolseley continues in wear to this day by most Canadian Infantry regiments.

A private of The Royal Canadian Regiment wearing the Regiment's full dress Wolseley in 2008 (Courtesy the Department of National Defence).

A 1913 dated Canadian Wolseley without puggaree (Courtesy of Clive M. Law).

The interior of the 1913 dated Wolseley shown on the previous page. The manufacturer is the Canadian firm of Anderson-MacBeth. Note the C over the broad arrow stamp indicating Canada (Courtesy of Clive M. Law).

Officers and men of the Royal Canadian Artillery at Camp Petawawa learning to lay the guns. The RCA flash, approved by Circular Letter in 1937, can be clearly seen on the officer's helmet far right. To his immediate front two Gunners are wearing the Hawley helmet which was a pressed fibre substitute for the Wolseley (Courtesey Clive M. Law).

A typical white parade helmet, this one belonging to the Regimental Band of the Royal Montreal Regiment (Collection of Clive M. Law).

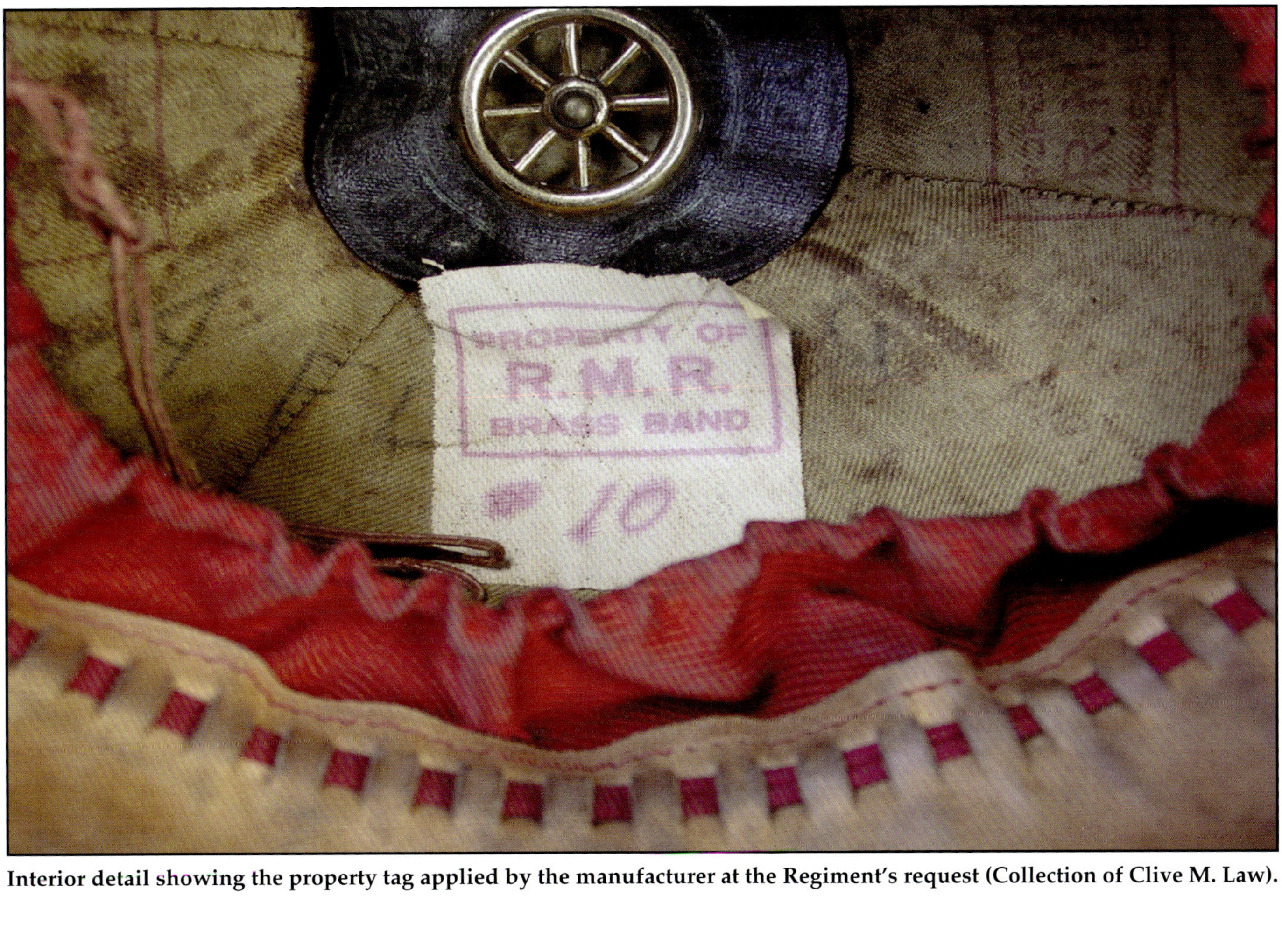

Interior detail showing the property tag applied by the manufacturer at the Regiment's request (Collection of Clive M. Law).

A pre-1968 Wolseley helmet to the Royal Canadian Ordnance Corps. The helmet features a certain "economy" attitude in that the ball and cup are made of chromed plastic and the puggaree is made of a canvas tape (Collection of Clive M. Law).

Interior detail of the Ordnance helmet above showing it as formerly belonging to the Royal Canadian Ordnance Corps Band at the Longue Pointe Ordnance Depot, Montreal (Collection of Clive M. Law).

A 1914 dated helmet to The Royal Canadian Regiment. This helmet features a distinctive removable puggaree (Collection of Clive M. Law).

The removable puggaree of The Royal Canadian Regiment helmet above. It shows the white backing to which the puggaree was sewn thereby allowing the helmet to be whitened without risk to the puggaree. The Regiment's badge is affixed to the puggaree. Note the anachronistic use of the Guelphic Crown and the cypher of Queen Victoria, Empress of India (Collection of Clive M. Law).

A Wolseley helmet to the 38th Battalion, Canadian Expeditionary Force. This unit is perpetuated by the Cameron Highlanders of Ottawa. The helmet features a collar badge in lieu of the usual cap badge (Collection of the Regimental Museum of the Cameron Highlanders of Ottawa, photo courtesy Clive M. Law).

A sentry of The Royal Canadian Regiment in Bermuda, 1915, wearing a khaki cover to his helmet (Courtesy of The Regimental Museum of The Royal Canadian Regiment).

An officer of the Royal Canadian Engineers, circa 1912. The RCE wore a white puggaree with the Corps badge to the front (Collection of Clive M. Law).

This helmet has an unidentified flash. Flashes came into general useage in the mid 1930s but were out of common use by the end of the Second World War (Collection of the Museum of Regiments, photo courtesy Clive M. Law).

This helmet became, for several years, the tradional hand-over gift from out-going Colonel to in-coming Colonel of the Manitoba Dragoons. It features the Regimental flash and cap badge (Collection of the Regimental Museum of the Manitoba Dragoons, photo courtesy Clive M. Law).

The Royal Winnipeg Rifles featured a multi-coloured puggaree, however no authority for this unique style appears to have either been sought by the regiment or approved by higher authorities (Collection of the Regimental Museum of the Royal Winnipeg Rifles, photo courtesy Clive M. Law).

The full dress Wolseley helmet of an officer of the Royal Canadian Army Medical Corps, circa 1950. The helmet features the ball and cup, gilt curb chain and gilt badge, centered on a white puggaree (Collection of Regimental Museum of the Governor General's Foot Guards, photo courtesy Clive M. Law).

The Governor General's Foot Guards followed the lead of their allied British regiment, the Coldstream Guards, and wore a scarlet plume. It is interesting to note that the plume is affixed to the left hand side whereas the Coldstreams wear theirs to the right (Collection of the Regimental Museum of the Governor General's Foot Guards, photo courtesy Clive M. Law).

A Major of the Stormont, Dundas and Glengarry Highlanders (The Glengarrians) wearing a tartan flash on his Wolseley. The other two soldiers are wearing the Hawley pressed fibre helmet (Collection of Clive M. Law).

The red and yellow flash of the Prince Edward Island Light Horse was also worn, painted, on the Mark II steel helmet in the early days of the Second World War (Collection and photo courtesy of the Regimental Museum of the Prince Edward Island Regiment).

A Wolseley helmet in the livery of the Royal Hamilton Light Infantry Regiment (Collection of the Base Museum, CFB Gagetown, photo courtesy of Clive M. Law).

Exhibiting the red hackle and a flash in Government tartan this helmet was the property of a junior officer of the Black Watch of Canada (Collection and photo courtesy of Pierre Price).

A modern day helmet in the colours of the Royal New Brunswick Regiment. Although the puggaree is of cloth the spike is of plastic (Collection of the Base Museum, CFB Gagetown, photo courtesy of Clive M. Law).

The French Grey flash identifies this helmet as worn by an officer of the Princess Patricia's Canadian Light Infantry (Collection of the Museum of Regiments, photo courtesy Clive M. Law).

A Model 1902 Wolseley to the Royal Canadian Horse Artillery. Attributed to driver Ethert Clair Lutes who joined the CEF in Moncton, New Brunswick in 1916 and served in France with the 65th Battery Canadian Field Artillery, RCHA. He was discharged as wounded in 1918 (Collection of Tony Schnurr).

The interior of the CEF Artillery Wolseley (Collection of Tony Schnurr).

A close-up of the Montreal maker's ink stamp to the interior of the CEF Artillery helmet showing the maker's name of William Scully and the date of 1916 (Collection of Tony Schnurr).

A Canadian-made version of the four seam Wolseley helmet dated 1942.

A close-up of the Montreal maker's ink stamp to the interior of the four seam helmet showing the maker's name of William Scully and the date of 1942. Note especially the "NAVAL" stamp which corresponds with the two Royal Australian Navy examples shown previously.

NEWFOUNDLANDERS IN TRAINING.
Eight weeks after the declaration of war five hundred Newfoundlanders embarked for England to complete training. Ninety-eight per cent. were Newfoundland born.

SUN HELMETS FOR WEAR IN GALLIPOLI.
" Just the men I want for the Dardanelles," Lord Kitchener said; and on August 15th, 1915, the 1st Battalion of Newfoundlanders left for Gallipoli.

Chapter 6
South African Wolseleys

Prior to the Union of South Africa in 1910, which was created from the Cape and Natal colonies, as well as the former Boer Republics of Orange Free State and Transvaal, there were separate armies for each of these four provinces. And while each of these provinces followed British military direction, the uniforms varied greatly. However, various units of these armies wore Wolseleys; for example, the Transvaal Cycle Corps (1905-1909) and the Cape Mounted Rifles (1902-1922). However, in 1909 the Transvaal Cycle Corps, renamed the Transvaal Cycle and Motor Corps, changed to a slouch hat.

The Defence Act of 1912 established a Union Defence Force (UDF) that included a Permanent Force of career soldiers, and an Active Citizen Force (ACF) of temporary conscripts and volunteers. The 1912 law required white males between seventeen and sixty years of age to serve in the military, but this law was not strictly adhered to, as there were also a large numbers of volunteers. Instead, a substantial proportion of white males aged from seventeen to twenty-five were drafted by lots into the ACF.

The 1923 UDF Uniform Instructions prescribed a Wolseley helmet in the veldt green colour. However not all units were dressed according to these regulations and some opted for khaki (veldt drab) instead.

The Wolseley helmet seems to have begun its decline when in 1930 the South African Air Force adopted the signature polo helmet, which was considered to be less cumbersome. In 1934 the change to polo helmets was signaled when army recruits were issued with both Wolseleys and polo pattern helmets. By December 1934 the Wolseley pattern was definitely considered to be obsolete as the new Permanent Force Dress instructions make no mention of it, and by 1935 polo helmets were probably in general use with Permanent Force units.

It seems that the polo helmets were considered better for the bush warfare waged by the South African forces and had been field tested during the Ipumba uprising of 1932. By 1935 the polo helmet was in general wear with the stocks of Wolseleys by then being exhausted. [27]

During the Second World War South African units relied primarily on the polo pattern helmets, and few if any Wolseley helmets were used by South African troops.

The South African Mounted Rifles (SAMR) were formed on 1 April 1913 from existing provincial Permanent and Police forces: the 1st Regiment was formed from the Cape Mounted Rifles, the 2nd from the Natal and Free State Police, the 3rd from the Natal Police, the 4th from the Transvaal Police and the 5th from the Cape Mounted Police. Until the start of WW1, the SAMR did policing work in many areas of South Africa. When WW1 started, the SAMR became the 6th Mounted Brigade. They served in German South West Africa and then returned to South Africa where many members were released to serve in the Overseas Expeditionary Forces. The remainder did policing duties in South Africa. In 1920, the disbandment of the force began. Most members then joined the newly formed South African Police. In 1926, the last regiment was disbanded (Courtesy of Col. William Endley).

The interior of the South African Mounted Rifles helmet. The headband has the standard eight cork spacers to provide ventilation around the headband. It was manufactured by E.W. Vero & Co. in 1921 who patented a detachable headband in 1925 (Courtesy of Col. William Endley).

The helmet badge of the South African Mounted Rifles. Note the initials of the unit in both English and Afrikaans (Courtesy of Col. William Endley).

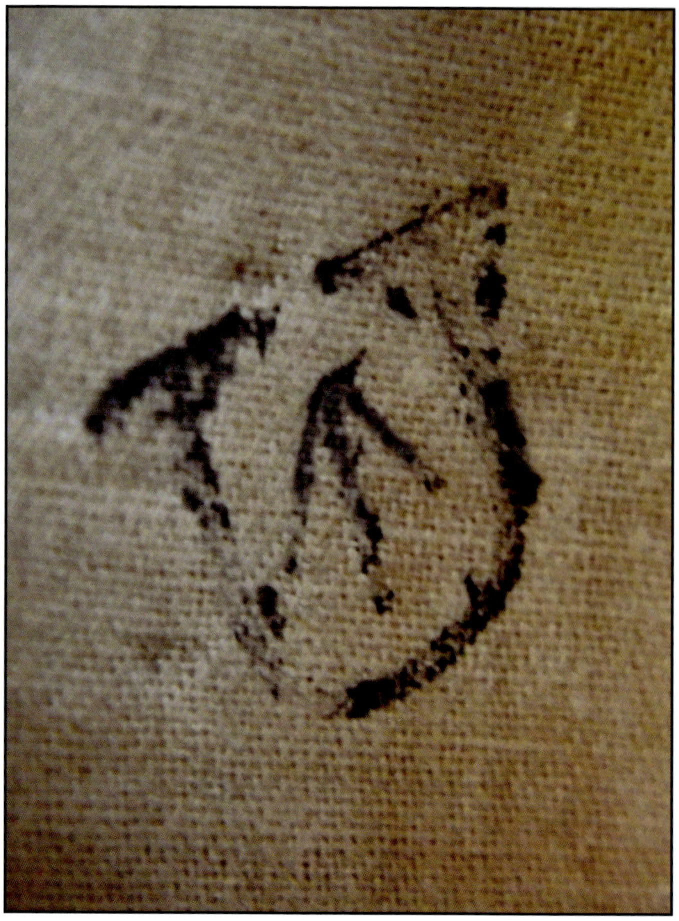

The War Office stamp to the South Africa Mounted Rifles with the "U" for Union Defence Force surrounding it. This was phased out in 1947/48 (Courtesy of Col. William Endley).

A trooper of the Cape Mounted Rifles 1913. This unit was originally formed as the Frontier Armed and Mounted Police in 1858. It was a para-military unit whose function was to maintain law and order along the Cape Colony's borders, and in 1878 was renamed the Cape Mounted Rifles as a unit of the Colonial Forces in South Africa. In 1913 the C.M.R. units were merged with the South African Mounted Rifles as the 1st SAMR. (Courtesy of Chris Boonzaier).

The maker's label of E.W. Vero & Co. to the interior of the South African Mounted Rifles helmet showing the date of 1921 (Courtesy of Col. William Endley).

The helmet flash of the South African Mounted Rifles from 1922 (Courtesy of Col. Dudley Wall).

A helmet to the British South Africa Police, a Southern Rhodesian unit which served with the British and South African forces in German East Africa 1915-18 and was responsible for the capture of Schuckmansberg in German South West Africa 1914 (Courtesy Col. Dudley Wall).

The Interior of the British South Africa Police helmet (Courtesy Col. Dudley Wall).

The helmet badge of the British South Africa Police 1920 - 1950s (Courtesy Col. Dudley Wall).

The interior of the British South Africa Police helmet showing the government stamp of S.R.G. (Southern Rhodesian Government) and date of 1939 (Courtesy Col. Dudley Wall).

A splendid study of a sergeant of the Transvaal Horse Artillery. The flash was worn on both sides of the helmet but reversed for the sake of symmetry i.e. the white portion of the zig-zag always faced to the rear (Courtesy Col. Dudley Wall).

The flash of the Transvaal Horse Artillery as shown opposite on the Wolseley helmet (Courtesy Col. Dudley Wall).

The flash of the South African Engineers Corps (Courtesy Andrew Dinnes).

The flash of the Natal Mounted Rifles, possibly World War I (Courtesy Andrew Dinnes).

The flash of the 6th South African Infantry, East Africa, World War I (Courtesy Andrew Dinnes).

The flash of the Enslin's Horse, German South West Africa in World War I (Courtesy Andrew Dinnes).

The flash of the Natal Scottish, World War II (Courtesy Andrew Dinnes).

A Wolseley to the Natal Light Horse, a unit that served as part of the British forces during the First World War in German South West Africa (Courtesy Andrew Dinnes).

The interior to the Natal Light Horse Wolseley. There is a faint inked name "114 E W Tait 3 Troop C SQD NLH" to the inside of the crown. The maker is E.W. Vero & Co. (Courtesy Andrew Dinnes).

NCOs of the South African Air Force wearing Wolseleys in the early 1930s (Courtesy Col. Dudley Wall).

A guard turnout of the South African Air Force circa 1930s (Courtesy Col. Dudley Wall).

A helmet to the Natal Infantry showing the blue/black flash, on the right hand side, which was used between 1923 and 1945 (Courtesy Col. Will Endley).

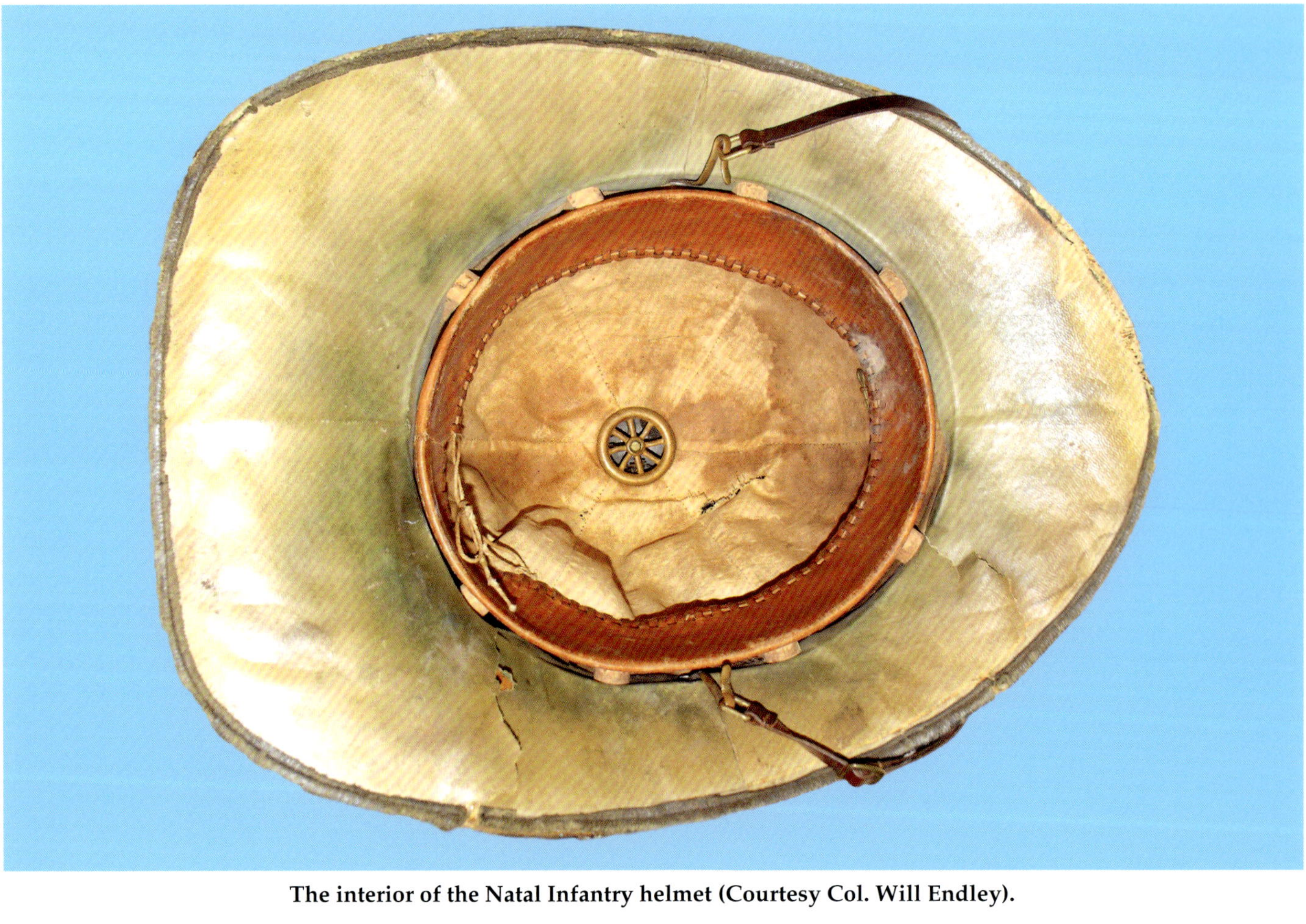

The interior of the Natal Infantry helmet (Courtesy Col. Will Endley).

A helmet to the Natal Infantry showing the blue/black flash, on the left hand side, which was used between 1923 and 1945 (Courtesy Col. Will Endley).

The front of the Natal Infantry Wolseley showing the "Universal" badge worn by a wide variety of units. The cloth backing to the badge is unidentified (Courtesy Col. Will Endley).

A Players Cigarette card showing a soldier of Regiment Louw Wepener in "veld green" uniform with Wolseley helmet circa 1934. This regiment belonged to the Orange Free State which was one of the four self-governing Colonies and which maintained its own Volunteers and Militia prior to the creation of the Union of South Africa in 1910.

The helmet flash of Regiment Louw Wepener. Note that the colours are reversed to the Player's representation. Black over yellow is the correct version (Courtesy of Col. Dudley Wall).

An example of a polo helmet which replaced the Wolseley in the middle 1930s. This one bears the badge of the South African Engineer Corps (Courtesy of Col. Dudley Wall).

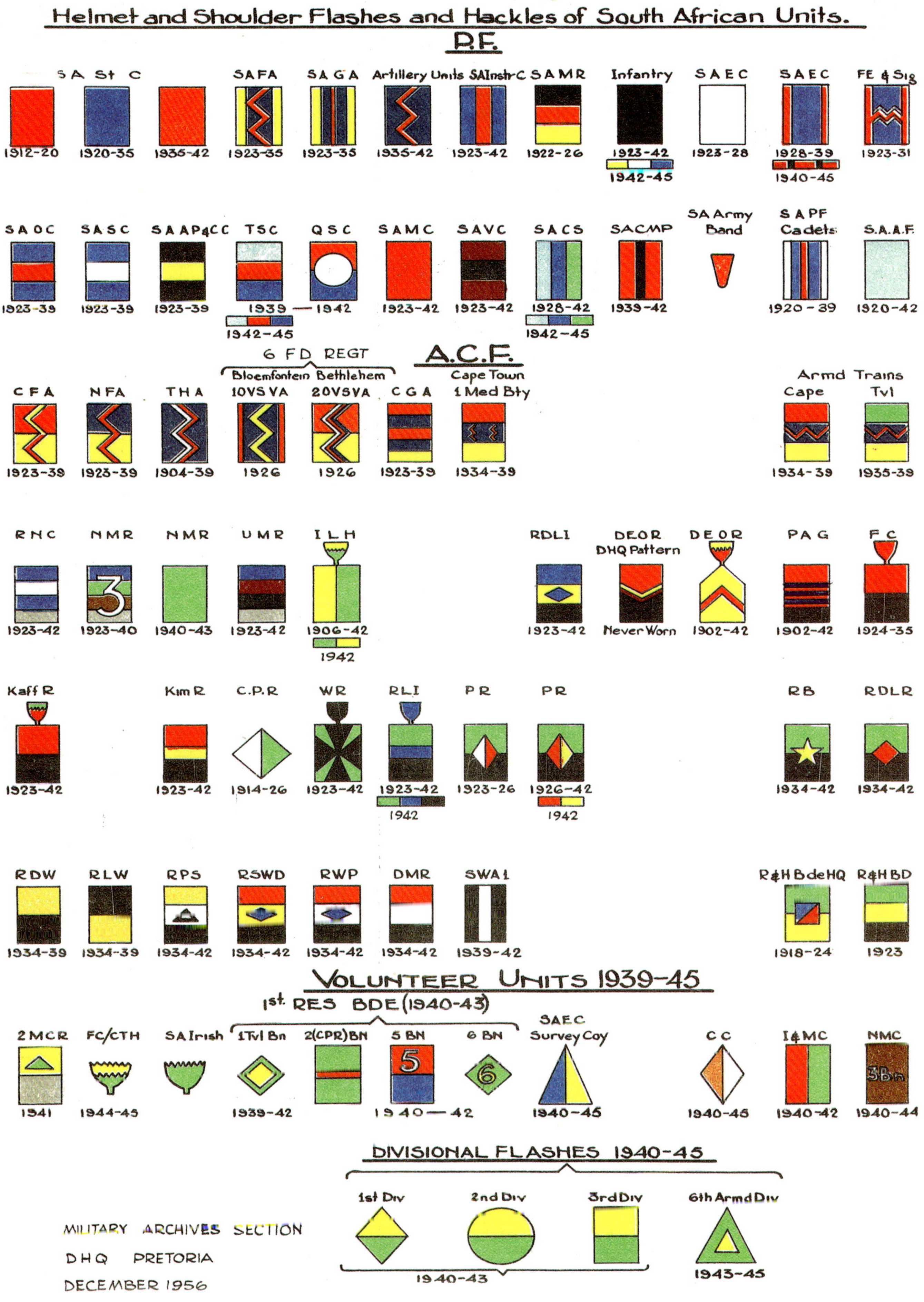

An official Union Defence Force poster of helmet, shoulder flashes and hackles 1923-1945 (Courtesy of Col. Dudley Wall).

Chapter 7
The Wolseley Helmet In Other Countries

While the Wolseley helmet saw service throughout the British Empire, the helmet pattern clearly inspired other military thinkers, and can be seen in similar designs from numerous nations, some of which continued to use the helmet pattern well into the latter part of the 20th century.

Originally the helmet wasn't so much copied, as it was imported. The British had sold Wolseley helmets to several powers in the years leading up to the First World War. The pattern was adopted, and in some cases modified - giving those helmets their own distinct take on the famous design.

Spain

Among the first powers to use the Wolseley helmet was Spain in the decade following the loss of much of its colonial empire in the Spanish-American War. Spain had been using a colonial pattern helmet, likely inspired by British and later French models. In 1909 the Spanish purchased a large number of Wolseley helmets from the British at Gibraltar. These helmets were used for the Spanish troops fighting in Morocco, and these were reported to have been white with a separate khaki cotton cover.

Apparently, the Spanish had liked the design so much that by 1912 a copy of the pattern was being produced in Spain. This helmet featured the same basic shape, but surviving examples show minor differences, notably that the Spanish added a side ventilation hole with a grommet on some models to help reduce the heat buildup to the wearer's head. The Spanish continued to use the Wolseley pattern, along with French purchased sun helmets, until 1917 when a khaki canvas brimmed hat known as the *Americano* replaced the Wolseley sun helmets.

Belgium and Ethiopia

At the beginning of the 20th century Belgium's colonial empire in Africa consisted of the personal fiefdom of Léopold II and was known as the Congo Free State. A private army, the Force Publique, which since the 1880s had used a uniform ill-suited to the climate, garrisoned this tropical land. Attempts to come up with a more practical uniform heightened over time, notably so when Belgium took over the administration of the Congo in 1908. By the outbreak of the First World War, the Belgian forces in Africa were wearing a khaki uniform and donning Wolseley helmets. The first of these were British made and supplied, but soon after the Belgians were making their own versions.

From the First World War through the Second World War these were worn with a lion rampant (in gilt for officers, silver for NCOs and bronze for other ranks) on

A Spanish made copy of the British Wolseley pattern. It features the same basic shape and design with some minor variations such as the side ventilation hole with grommet (Courtesy collection of Bill Combs).

The pattern of helmet adopted by the Belgians pre World War I which superseded the earlier 1880s pattern. This would appear to be a direct copy of the British Wolseley (Courtesy Peter Verstraeten-Vlerick) .

An Ethiopian cavalry helme, post-World War II.

the front of the helmet, below the tri-colour (red/yellow/black) national cockade. Following World War II the lion rampant was dropped, and this helmet was last used by the Belgian forces during the Congo Crisis of the early 1960s.

Belgium also supplied the helmet pattern to the army of Ethiopia, which had used a Wolseley helmet throughout the early 1930s prior to the invasion by Italian forces in 1935. When the nation obtained its independence, it once again used a Wolseley helmet, which were first imported from the U.K. as well as from the Belgian Congo, and later made in Ethiopia. These helmets, which typically had a badge of service device on the front as well as a tri-colour (green/yellow/red) cockade on the right hand side, were used until the early 1970s when the nation was gripped in a civil war.

Italy

The Italians never officially adopted the British Wolseley, but in the late 1920s the nation under the Fascists began to modernize its army. This included replacing the aging colonial pattern helmets, which had been in use since the late 1880s, with a new wide-brimmed helmet that was probably inspired by the Wolseley. The new helmet pattern, known as the Model 1928, was first used in the field during the Libyan uprising in 1931, but saw widespread use during the invasion of Ethiopia (1935-36).

The helmet, which features the same shape and profile, was made of cork and featured a rounded dome. It was covered in a thin cloth cover - usually khaki coloured cotton - and of six even panels. The cotton cloth seems thinner than that used on the British helmet and may have been a cost saving exercise on the part of the Italian helmet makers.

It featured a brim that was pointed at the front while the back brim curled up just slightly. The helmet was typically worn with an Italian tri-colour (red/white/green) cockade along with brass arm of service badge on the front of the helmet. Embroidered insignia may have also been worn, but likely to a far lesser extent. Additionally some units - notably those of a Fascist paramilitary nature - wore the helmet with just the metal device and without the tri-colour cockade. Unlike the British helmets, or those used by the other nations, the Italian helmets were typically worn without a puggaree.

The Italian Model 1928 helmets had three other notable differences from the true British Wolseley pattern. The first is that the ventilator cap was often a tan painted bare metal rather than the traditional cloth cover version found on almost all other sun helmets. These were usually of a non-ferrous metal, such as aluminium.

As noted earlier an exception to this rule was that the ventilator cap of the British Worcestershire Regiment Wolseley was painted green rather than having a cloth cover.

An example of the Italian M28 with the badge and feathers of the 8th Bersaglieri. Note the meshed ventilation hole to the side.

A variation of the Italian M28, made of straw probably as a result of wartime shortages of cork. It contains a liner, size stamp and the remnants of a maker's label, all suggesting that this was issued (or intended to be issued) without a fabric covering, rather than being an "unfinished" example. Only three examples are known to exist of this very rare helmet.

A highly romanticised Italian poster from the Second Italian-Abyssinian War (1935-36). It highlights Italian efforts to build a Neo-Roman empire.

The helmets also featured side vents - slightly larger than the size of a pencil eraser - that were covered with a mesh screen and grommet. The final major distinguishing feature of these helmets was the side pocket, which was provided for the wearing of feathers on the right side of the helmet. While this practice was typical of specialized units, such as the Bersaglieri troops, nearly every Italian helmet has this curious side pocket.

The Model 28 was produced in large numbers, and was used throughout Italy's colonies. However, it appears that the Italians were unable to produce the helmet in substantial enough amounts to meet the demands of Benito Mussolini's growing military forces in the tropics, as the Poliza Africa Italiana (Italian African Police) relied on large numbers of Anglo-Indian helmets. Additionally, prior to the outbreak of World War II, Italian officer's also utilized Anglo-Indian produced helmets, likely because they were of superior quality to the rudimentary Model 1928.

Greece

Although the Balkan nation of Greece lacked any "overseas" colonies, the nation did adopt sun helmets, beginning in the 1930s with a Wolseley style helmet. These were locally produced and were certainly based on the British design featuring a flared out brim with a pointed front visor. These helmets were made of cork and covered in cloth, which was whitened with blanco. Instead of a puggaree a thick band of canvas was wrapped

The Greek forces used a sun helmet based on the British Wolseley and these were introduced in the 1930s and remained in use until the 1970s. This example bears the Greek Air Force insignia of the late 1960s.

A side view of the Greek Wolseley.

A 1934 Portuguese officer's helmet featuring a puggaree and the gilt badge (Courtesy Pedro Soares Branco).

An example of a 1934 Portuguese Other Ranks helmet. Note the lack of a puggaree and any badge (Courtesy Pedro Soares Branco).

A 1913 Portuguese Naval Officer's helmet (Courtesy Pedro Soares Branco).

around the base of the dome. In addition to the vent at the top of the helmet, the Greek version also featured three vent holes with grommets on each side.

During the Second World War the German occupying forces used large numbers of captured Greek helmets, and these were especially popular with the Kriegsmarine.

The helmet pattern remained in use after the country was liberated. Throughout the Greek Civil War and during the Cold War, a variety of military badges were worn. The helmets were believed to be very popular with the Greek Air Force and these were used into the 1970s.

Portugal

Portugal had been one England's oldest allies, but the countries faced cracks in their relationship over African territorial ambitions in the late 19th century. The alliance between the nations was renewed during the First World War, and in Africa the Portuguese Army began to wear British Wolseley pattern helmets.

The Portuguese Navy had previously adopted a helmet in the Wolseley shape in 1913 for officers that featured a "light body," which was not cork but rather a glued cloth. This helmet was used until around 1925 when the navy adopted the French pattern sun helmet.

However, the army retained the Wolseley, and in 1934 a modified pattern was adopted. The officer version featured a puggaree wrapped around the helmet, while other ranks had a simple strip of cloth.

Over time, both patterns were worn by officers and the ranks, but it is believed that brass badges were worn by the ranks while officers wore gilt badges.

Although the Wolseley sun helmet was not used in the Portuguese territory of Goa in India, some officers did wear the Wolseley with the white summer uniform, and this practice seems to have begun around 1930.

Appendix - Khaki

Khaki is the Persian word for dust, and it was Harry Burnett Lumsden who, in 1849, introduced khaki as a dyed cloth for the Corps of Guides. [28] It was a drab grey colour rather than the yellowish-brown khaki which became universal for the British Army in the late 19th Century.

The British in India often fought in their summer whites and as Michael Barthorp says -

The [Indian] Mutiny saw the beginning of khaki in the British Army, and clothing in this colour, usually of a greyish hue... was widely adopted during its operations. Nevertheless, many re-inforcing battalions, sent out to the Mutiny from England, had to fight in their red or rifle-green until they could acquire more suitable clothing. Despite its popularity, khaki was abandoned after the Mutiny... Not until 1868 did khaki re-appear, when British regiments sent from India to Abyssinia again dyed their white clothing for the campaign. [29]

Over the years attempts were made to formulate a dye which would provide a khaki colour of consistency and longevity. These attempts failed with the uniforms varying greatly in colour after only a few weeks or months of exposure to the weather. It was commonplace for troops to stain their white uniforms and helmets with any appropriate substance in order to break up the white and therefore provide some camouflage. Such materials as mud, tea, coffee, tobacco juice and curry powder were used to a greater or lesser effect.

In 1884 the problem was solved when a fast-dye was patented which produced a consistent yellowish-brown colour over a prolonged period. As Paul Leuillot states in his essay *Frederic Zuber's visits to England, 1833-41* -

R.S. Crossley, Accrington Captains of Industry (Accrington 1930), pp.80-3: 'Frederick Steiner (born 30 March 1787; died 29 November 1869)',. Steiner became a naturalised British subject when he established his own firm in 1836 and bought Hyndburn House from the Peels c. 1849. He also invited to England the Alsatian Frederick Albert Gatty (1819-88), who founded a Turkey red dyeing firm in Accrington in 1843. Gatty improved the dyeing of Turkey red with garancine, for the manufacture of which Steiner took out a patent on 8 August 1843. He made 'Gatty red' famous in Eastern markets. Finally, he discovered the mineral khaki dye which he produced by using oxides of chromium and iron and which he patented on 20 August 1884. [30]

It is interesting to note that a ledger kept by the Royal Clothing Factory records a change in the cotton khaki drill material. This was dated as February 1924 and further notes indicate that it was a colour change. It would appear that the new shade was very slightly greener than the one it replaced. [31]

Henceforth, the British Army could present a "uniform" front to its enemies and "white uniforms" were the province of full dress ceremonial occasions.

Glossary

ACI Army Council Instruction. The Army Council was the Army's senior "management board" and issued ACIs weekly, each one identified with a number and the year e.g. ACI1248/1938.

Bersaglieri An elite body of Italian troops fulfilling the role of light infantry and shock troops. The term is loosely translated as English Marksmen.

Buckram A stiffened cotton material used for corrugated ventilation between the helmet shell and the leather headband.

Cawnpore The Cawnpore Tent Club Helmet was a helmet made of pith, usually with a quilted cotton covering, used to supplement the Wolseley for other than full dress occasions.

Chinchain A metal device of interlinked loops used to secure the helmet to the wearer's head. Worn on ceremonial occasions.

Chinstrap A leather strap, fixed to the interior of the helmet by brass hooks. Used to secure the helmet to the wearer's head but more often worn looped up over the front peak.

CMR Cape Mounted Rifles.

Cockade A knot of ribbons, or other circular or oval shaped symbol of distinctive colours.

Doeskin A very fine woollen cloth originating from Melton Mowbray, Leicestershire.

Dress Regulations A publication produced by the British Army, via the H.M.S.O., providing precise instructions and definitions for officers' equipment and uniforms.

Flash Usually a cloth insignia affixed to the puggaree to identify the battalion/regiment/corps.

Flip The point at which the puggaree is turned over. Normally only front and rear but some regiments had three or four such flips.

Foil Tin or aluminium foil used to provide cooling within the helmet.

Full Dress Occasions when the Full Dress uniform, as opposed to active duty etc., was to be worn.

GCB The Most Honourable Order of the Bath (formerly The Most Honourable Military Order of the Bath) is a British order of chivalry founded by George I on 18 May 1725.

GCMG The Most Distinguished Order of Saint Michael and Saint George is a British order of chivalry founded on 28 April 1818 by George, Prince Regent (later George IV).

Hackle A "shaving brush" embellishment of cut feather or horse or goat's hair of the regimental colours and inserted between the helmet and the puggaree.

High-hook A small hook used when the chinchain was looped up rather than being worn under the chin. Usually fixed to the top rear of the helmet crown or fixed to the spike base if fitted.

H.M.S.O. Her/His Majesty's Stationery Office.

Japanning A process of lacquering a metal storage/transit tin.

Khaki A yellowish-brown colour used to provide camouflage to uniforms Prior to a fast dye being developed, in 1884 by Gatty, tea, mud, coffee, curry powder, etc., were used to colour the white items of uniform. Frederick Albert Gatty, came to England from Alsace, and founded a dyeing firm in Acrington in 1843. He discovered the mineral khaki dye which he produced by using oxides of chromium and iron and which he patented on 20 August 1884.

Khaki Solar Pith Hat The headgear that officially replaced the Wolseley in 1938, but which had been used in conjunction with the Wolseley since the early 1930s.

KP The Most Illustrious Order of Saint Patrick is a British order of chivalry associated with Ireland.

List of Changes These lists were issued monthly and were published by the War Department. They advised of changes in all military stores, ranging from bayonets to bicycles, hospital furniture to howitzers etc.

NLH Natal Light Horse.

OM The Order of Merit is an order recognizing distinguished service in the armed forces, science, art, literature, or for the promotion of culture. Established in 1902 by King Edward VII.

Pagri See puggaree.

PC A member of Her Majesty's Most Honourable Privy Council.

Piping one or more coloured pleats inserted into the puggaree. Usually of silk or woollen cloth.

Pleats The number of folds or pleats of a puggaree. Ranging from 3 to 12.

Plumes Usually swan feathers attached to the top of the helmet and used on ceremonial occasions.

Private Purchase The system whereby officers were required to purchase their own uniforms and equipment.

Puggaree a strip of cloth wound around the base of the crown of the helmet, thought to provide protection from the sun and sword cuts. There are many spellings of this Hindi word, including "paggari" or "pagri", which translate loosely as small turban.

RAOC Royal Army Ordnance Corps. Responsible for supply/storage of necessaries to the army.

RASC Royal Army Service Corps. Responsible for transport and supply. It provided the daily needs of the soldier, by supplying food, ammunition, petrol and lubricants, for all normal and battle requirements. It was also responsible for battlefield recovery of damaged/broken-down vehicles.

RCHA Royal Canadian Horse Artillery.

RTC Royal Tank Corps.

RTR Royal Tank Regiment.

SAMR South African Mounted Rifles.

Sealed Pattern The pattern of equipment which all manufacturers were required to use for items supplied to the army.

Shikari A civilian helmet much used in hunting, both by the military and civilians.

Short Service 6 years active and 6 years reserve service.

Slider Badge A helmet badge that has a shank that slides between the puggaree and the helmet shell.

Sola pith the original material used for sun helmets. From the flowering plant *Aeschynomene asper* or other species of the *Fabaceae* family. Sola soon became Anglicised to Solar.

VD The Volunteer Officers' Decoration was created by Royal Warrant under command of Queen Victoria on 25 July 1892 to reward 'efficient and capable' officers of the Volunteer Force who had served for twenty years.

Ventilation The various methods employed to allow air to circulate within the helmet to provide cooling.

Ventilation Cap The small zinc "button" usually covered in khaki drill which screwed into the top of the helmet and provided air flow via three holes.

Visor an extension to the front of a helmet to provide protection from the sun.

Vocabulary of Clothing and Neccessaries Lists of officially existing items of clothing etc., that are available to the British Army.

Notes

1. Hannah, W.H., *Bob's, Kipling's General. The Life of Field Marshal Earl Roberts of Kandahar, VC*, Leo Cooper, 1972.
2. *Dress Regulations for the Army, 1900*, David & Charles (Publishers) Limited, Devon, 1970.
3. Mollo, John, *The Formation Sign*, The Military Heraldry Society, FS203, July-Sept., 2001.
4. Barthorp, M, *British Infantry Uniforms Since 1660*, Blandford Press, Dorset, 1982.
5. Haythornthwaite, P.J., *The Boer War, Uniforms Illustrated #19*, Arms and Armour Press, Dorset, 1987.
6. Mollo, John, *The Formation Sign,* The Military Heraldry Society, FS147, July-Sept., 1987.
7. *Bosley's Auction Catalogue*, item 861, 3rd June 2009.
8. Suciu, Peter with Stuart Bates, *Military Sun Helmets of the World*, Service Publications, Ottawa, 2009.
9. *Dress Regulations for the Army 1904*, H.M.S.O., 1904.
10. *Dress Regulations for the Army 1911*, Tharston Press, Norfolk, 1986.
11. www.HowStuffWorks.com
12. Davis, Brian, *British Army Uniforms and Insignia of World War Two*, Book Club Associates, London, 1983.
13. *Royal Army Ordnance Corps Gazette*, April, 1937.
14. Change B4689, *List of Changes*, 30/5/41.
15. Change B6960, *List of Changes* ,14th Aug., 1942.
16. Harfield, A.G., *Headdress, Badges and Embellishments of the Royal Corps of Signals*, Picton Publishing Wiltshire,1982.
17. *Regulations for the Clothing of the Army 1914*, H.M.S.O. reprint by Naval and Military Press, East Sussex, England.
18. Mills, Jon, *From Scarlet to Khaki*, Wardens Publishing, Kent, 2005.
19. Change B4689, *List of Changes*, 30/5/41.
20. Change B6499, *List of Changes*, 31/7/42.
21. Renbourn, E.T., *Life and Death of the Solar Topi, Journal of Tropical Medicine and Hygiene, Vol. 65*, August, 1962.
22. Davis, Brian, *British Army Uniforms and Insignia of World War Two*, Book Club Associates, London, 1983.
23. Payne, Peter and Jim MacDonald, *Tanks Again*, Self published CD.
24. Mollo, John, *The Formation Sign,* The Military Heraldry Society, FS158, April-June, 1990.
25. Change C4433, *List of Changes*, 28th Feb, 1951.
26. Wilkinson-Latham, Robert, *The Royal Navy 1790-1970*, Osprey Publishing Ltd, 1977.
27. Paterson, Hamish, *South Africa's Second World War Bush Warfare Uniform*, South African National Museum of Military History.
28. Carman, W.Y., *Indian Army Uniforms*, Morgan-Grampian, London, 1969.
29. Barthorp, M, *British Infantry Uniforms Since 1660*, Blandford Press, Dorset, 1982.
30. Ratcliffe, Barrie M., *Great Britain and Her World, 1750-1914: Essays in Honour of W.O.Henderson*, Manchester University Press, 1975.
31. Army Clothing Department: Register of Changes (National Archives File WO359), Feb. 1924.

Bibliography

Abbott, Peter, *Armies of East Africa 1914 -18*, Osprey Publishing, Oxford, 2002

Abbott, Peter, *Colonial Armies Africa 1850 to 1918*, Foundry Books, Nottingham, 2006

Army Clothing Department: Register of Changes (National Archives File WO359), 14th June, 1921.

Army Clothing Department: Register of Changes (National Archives File WO359), Feb. 1924.

Branco, Pedro Soares, *Coberturas Militares Portuguesas: 1740-1918*, Edições Inapa, 2000.

Barthorp, M, *British Infantry Uniforms Since 1660*, Blandford Press, Dorset, 1982.

Bosley's Auction Catalogue, item 861, 3rd June 2009.

Carman, W.Y., *Indian Army Uniforms*, Morgan-Grampian, London, 1969.

Chappell, Mike, *The British Soldier in the 20th Century Field Service Headdress 1902 to the Present Day*, Wessex Military Publishing, Devon, 1987.

Chappell, Mike, *The British Soldier in the 20th Century Tropical Uniforms*, Wessex Military Publishing, Devon, 1988.

Davis, Brian L., *British Army Uniforms and Insignia of World War Two*, Book Club Associates, London, 1983.

Dress Regulations for the Army, 1900, David & Charles (Publishers) Limited, Devon, 1970.

Dress Regulations for the Army 1904, H.M.S.O., 1904.

Dress Regulations for the Army 1911, Tharston Press, Norfolk, 1986.

Hannah, W.H., *Bob's, Kipling's General. The Life of Field Marshal Earl Roberts of Kandahar, VC*, Leo Cooper, 1972.

Harfield, A.G., *Headdress, Badges and Embellishments of the Royal Corps of Signals*, Picton Publishing Wiltshire,1982.

Haythornthwaite, P.J., *The Boer War, Uniforms Illustrated #19*, Arms and Armour Press, Dorset, 1987.

Change B4689, *List of Changes*, 30/5/41.

Change B6960, *List of Changes*, 14th Aug., 1942.

Marzetti, Paolo, *Elmetti/Helmets*, Parma, 2003

Mills, Jon, *From Scarlet to Khaki*, Wardens Publishing, Kent, 2005.

Mollo, John, *The Formation Sign*, The Military Heraldry Society, FS147, July-Sept., 1987.

Mollo, John, *The Formation Sign*, The Military Heraldry Society, FS158, April-June, 1990.

Mollo, John, *The Formation Sign*, The Military Heraldry Society, FS203, July-Sept., 2001.

Payne, Peter and Jim MacDonald, *Tanks Again*, Self published CD.

Players, John & Sons, *Military Uniforms of the British Empire*

Ratcliffe, Barrie M., *Great Britain and Her World, 1750-1914: Essays in Honour of W.O.Henderson*, Manchester University Press, 1975.

Regulations for the Clothing of the Army 1914, H.M.S.O. reprint by Naval and Military Press, East Sussex, England.

Renbourn, E.T., *Life and Death of the Solar Topi, Journal of Tropical Medicine and Hygiene, Vol. 65*, August, 1962.

Royal Army Ordnance Corps Gazette, April, 1937.

Simpkins, Major B.G., *Rand Light Infantry*, Howard Timmins, Cape Town, S.A., 1965.

Suciu, Peter with Stuart Bates, *Military Sun Helmets of the World*, Service Publications, Ottawa, 2009.

Wall, Dudley, *Starting out Collecting South African Militaria*, Second Edition, Self Published, 2005.

Wilkinson-Latham, Robert and Christopher, *Infantry Uniforms Book Two 1855-1939*, Blandford Press, London, 1970.

www.HowStuffWorks.com

INDEX

Index

Dedicated to my late father, Harold Bates, 1919-2008.
Just a good man.